Are you here in this hell too?

Memories of troubled times
1944 - 1945

Are you here in this hell too?

Memories of Troubled Times
1944 - 1945

Elisabeth Sommer-Lefkovits

Translation from the German
Marjorie Harris

Introduction by Elaine Feinstein

The Menard Press
1995

Are you here in this hell too?
Memories of Troubled Times, 1944 - 1945
Elisabeth Sommer-Lekovits

© 1995 Elisabeth Sommer-Lefkovits
Translated from the German by Marjorie Harris
English translation © 1995 The Menard Press

Cover design by Audrey Jones
Design, setting and camera ready copy by Lijna Minnet

We would like to thank Chronos Verlag Zürich for technical help

Picture attribution:
Photographs 1 - 6, 38 - 41: in private hands
Photographs 7 - 37: Imperial War Museum, London

Representation and distribution in UK:
Central Books (Troika)
99 Wallis Road
Hackney Wick
London E9 5LN
Tel: 0181-986 4854

Distribution in the rest of the world apart from North America:
Central Books

Distribution in North America:
SPD Inc
1814 San Pablo Avenue
Berkeley
CA 94702
USA

ISBN: 1 874320 11 X

The Menard Press
8 The Oaks
Woodside Avenue
London N12 8AR
Tel: 0181-446 5571

Printed at Alden Press
Oxford and Northampton

Contents

Page

Introduction

This is in many ways a unique memoir. It is the only first hand account I know of a mother's efforts to preserve the life of her child in the full horror of the Camps. Written without the least literary flourish, and concerned only to speak simply and honestly of that experience, this is necessarily a bleak and frightening story, yet I finished reading it without the usual sense of hopelessness.

It is more than a quarter of a century now since I first met Dr Ivan Lefkovits in the charming house in a leafy part of Basel where he lived with his wife and children. I remember Ivan's expression then as particularly open and friendly, with the same round trusting eyes as my youngest son. Ivan was one of the founding scientists at the Hoffman La Roche Institute for Immunological Research at which my husband was working for six months, and we saw a good deal of him. I can recall discussing the anti-Semitism of the Slansky trials with him – he was a Czech, I understood – and recall his comments on the Soviet habit of putting Jewish leaders in charge of unpopular regimes. At no time did I guess that he and his remarkable mother had been prisoners in Ravensbrück and Bergen-Belsen.

After I had read this manuscript, I was puzzled by his reticence, since Mrs Sommer-Lefkovits makes clear that he had encouraged her to write the memoir in the last years of her life. I asked him on the telephone why he had never mentioned his experiences either to my husband or myself. He could only say that it was a question of either never speaking of such events or talking of them all the time.

Mrs Sommer-Lefkovits went into hiding in September 1944 in Slovakia. At this time Mrs Lefkovits was protected by her useful occupation as a pharmacist, both her children were hidden in an orphanage, and the Germans were already beginning to lose the war. After the Slovak uprising, however, the Nazis began to round up and deport all Jews whatever occupations they had. A Slovak friend was brave enough to warn Mrs Lefkovits and another took the risk of hiding her as others had earlier tried to smuggle her two sons across the border to what seemed then to be the safety of Hungary. Inevitably mother and children were soon caught, and those who had helped them were deported with them. The details of their attempts to escape are enormously touching, particularly the portrait of Ivan as a small boy learning sign language in order to pass as deaf and dumb, and the separation from the elder son Paul is heartbreaking. That Mrs Lefkovits managed to endure until the liberation of Bergen-Belsen in 1945 is a happy ending of a kind, even though so many of their family ended in mass graves.

Their survival was a matter in large part of late capture, and some who were less fortunate died even after liberation, since the English soldiers were ignorant of the dangers of ordinary food for those suffering from starvation; and knowing as much ensures there is no comfortable moral to be drawn from a tale of courage and endurance. Mrs Lefkovits' story is told in clean spare language, without the least attempt to mitigate or exaggerate, and without fudging her occasional lapses of memory. No-one who reads it will fail to be moved.

Elaine Feinstein

Instead of a Prologue

For a time there were fifty copies of my "*Memories of Troubled Times, 1944-1945*". I can still count up the recipients of the book. I was quite amazed that the book had been read outside my circle of friends and had found favour. This 'second wave' reacted with letters and telephone calls. Some needed to tell me what they themselves had suffered during the war, others to comment on my fate and there were others who simply wanted to know what had happened to us afterwards.

In the summer of 1993, Mr Ewald Billerbeck, a long-standing contributor to the '*Basler Zeitung*', visited me frequently, and on 12 October a book review by him appeared in the paper.*

The reactions of '*Basler Zeitung*' readers finally destroyed any doubts I had had about whether it was worth describing in writing the horrors which I and my then seven- and fourteen- year old children had undergone. I realised that it is right to leave these lines behind. There are six million people who are not able to speak for themselves, so it is even more important that the living do it for them. There are individuals or political groups who deny the existence of The Holocaust. Any survivor who remains silent allows those who deny it to be heard.

The events I am describing are a revelation of experiences I have not been able to talk about. The wounds remained unhealed after the war and we did not want to reopen the scars. My son never speaks of his experiences, although he remembers a great deal, as I do, and the next generation, meaning my grandson, knows very little. Wolf Biermann once said: "He who does not know where he comes from, does not know where he is going". So I am also telling this story for my grandson, for my friends, for all those who want to know about yesterday's holocaust and who want to stop tomorrow's holocaust from happening. I must stress that I am not describing "The Holocaust", just a small part of it. "The Holocaust" defies description – from my experience and in my opinion it was a unique event, with which it is very difficult to draw parallels with other human tragedies.

But my fate, and the fate of my family, those were (are)

experiences which repeat themselves day after day – in Somalia, in Bosnia – and we sit and watch helpless (on TV) and do nothing as disaster unfolds.

Elisabeth Sommer-Lefkovits

* see Afterword

1.   Elisabeth Lefkovits, Graduate in Pharmacy, 1926

2.   My mother, Anna Strausz-Horowitz, 1872 - 1945

3.   My father, Sigmund Strausz, 1867 - 1934

4.   Myself, with Paul and Ivan.

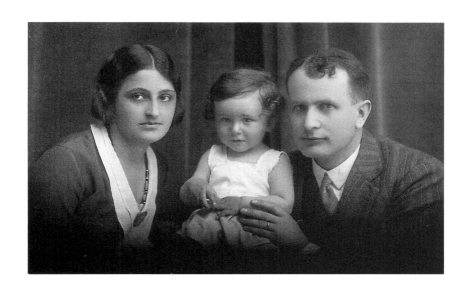

5. Myself, Paul and my husband, Dr Desider Lefkovits (c. 1933). Paul was taken from me in Ravensbrück Concentration Camp. I never saw him again.

6. My niece Katica Fésüs, aged 7, shot by the SS near Kremnica.

September 1944

It is a beautiful, warm summer's day.

I am trying to prepare myself to cope with all the heavy duties I have to undertake. I am Jewish, with a diploma in pharmacy, which puts me in a 'reserved occupation', and I am employed at the Pfeiler Pharmacy in Presov. Apart from me, there are two other colleagues who hold diplomas, and two technicians. We are very busy, because, apart from the clientèle from the town, we also have another very important and nerve-wracking duty to perform.

Even before the national uprising against the Nazi regime in Slovakia in August 1944, we had begun to supply the partisans with medication, bandages and disinfectants in ever greater quantities. However, this had to be done very carefully and in the greatest secrecy, so that neither partisans nor we pharmacists put ourselves in danger. At that time even the smallest assistance to the partisans was punishable by death.

The order was brought secretly into the pharmacy in an envelope by an unknown member of the resistance, mostly when several customers were present, so that it was difficult to see who had put it there. The completed order was then collected unobtrusively. Even we, the members of staff, were hardly aware of when and by whom the order had been collected. In the event of any of us being arrested and questioned, none of us could betray another.

That's how things were till 11 September, 1944.

A few weeks later, as I lay on the straw-covered cement floor of the Gestapo prison, I had all day and night to mull over whether our dangerous aid to the partisans, carried out so meticulously and carefully, had been known to the Gestapo all the time.

One sunny morning, Mrs Kissoczy, wife of the well-known and respected Presov doctor, came in to the crowded pharmacy. She came straight to my counter and asked me in a calm, quiet tone for aspirin. It was unusual for a relative of the doctor, in whose practice hundreds of different medicines were stored, to come into a pharmacy and buy aspirin.

As I handed her the small packet of aspirin, as requested, she bent her head as if talking to her purse, and whispered "Disappear right away; the Gestapo are now arresting all the Jewish doctors and pharmacists who are still here", and she quietly left the shop.

With a calm movement I put my fountain pen into its usual holder (we didn't have ballpoint pens in those days), went to the back to take off my overall, and made to leave the shop by the main door. At that very moment, two men from the Gestapo, accompanied by a Hlinka guardsman, entered the pharmacy. In a loud and vigorous voice one of them shouted "Heil Hitler! We are looking for the Jewess, Elisabeth Lefkovits".

My colleagues did not betray that the Jewess they were looking for had just left the pharmacy with the lie "I'll be back in a minute".

I kept sufficient presence of mind to be able to warn the vet, Dr Benedek, who I happened to meet in the street at that moment, of the imminent danger. Thanks to my warning, the Benedek family was able to escape.

So began seven frightening weeks of a life in hiding for me and my children.

Katica and the orphanage

This 'final purge' by the Gestapo, after the Slovak national uprising, caught us unawares. Since the main deportation in 1942, we had over-estimated the apparent state of peace and taken our relatively comfortable existence as Jews 'necessary to the economy' too much for granted. The Russians seemed to be making such victorious headway, that we never imagined at the time that another round of deportations was on the cards, and had made no preparations for a life on the run.

As I left work on 11 September, 1944, after Mrs Kissoczy's kind warning, I had no idea where to go next. I only knew that I could not go back to my flat where I had been living temporarily, since the Gestapo would be looking for me there.

No-one would have guessed from my apparently calm demeanour that I felt like a hunted wild animal. I didn't know which direction to take, where to go, who to turn to for help.
I reached a house on the corner of the main road (then called Hinkova Street) and suddenly noticed, as if all my steps had been led by a supernatural force, that I was standing in front of a house, the rear part of which belonged to Katica Svaton, a very dear, friendly, 'Aryan', unmarried dressmaker. She was loved by all the families in whose houses she worked. After momentary reflection, I tried my luck. She was at home!

She was visibly troubled when I described my position. We were both at a loss and in despair. We couldn't think of anyone who would give me shelter, at least temporarily. I couldn't even consider asking any 'Aryans' who had children, or unreliable neighbours. In the meantime night had fallen, and shortly afterwards the air raid sirens went off. Mrs Svaton gave me something to eat and we discussed the possibilities for finding refuge.

"Your children are safe at the moment, and we will find a solution for you", said Mrs Svaton. "Stay with me. I'll put you in my bed, with the blinds open, so that the neighbours don't get suspicious about me hiding anyone. I'll put food at the end of the bed. Don't get out of bed all day." With a "goodnight", she ended her instructions, and we went to sleep.

To sleep. . . I couldn't get to sleep although I was exhausted. Surely I couldn't stay in bed here, cut off from my children and from all knowledge of what was going on, which was so vital for my survival. Then I did fall asleep.

In the morning I awoke, put myself and the old-fashioned feather-bed to rights and slipped back into bed. The camouflage of the big empty bedroom was complete. With open eyes I lay in the half-light, the path in front of the windows only three or four paces away from me.

My thoughts returned constantly to my two children, Paul and Ivan. From time to time the peace and quiet in the house were broken. Footsteps on the path came nearer and then went on past. My thoughts were fixed on the family all the time. Perhaps my dearest ones were being cared for as well as I was. My husband lay in a hospital bed in far-off Budapest, but hospitals offered a certain safety, or so I thought. No-one would be deported from there. Hospitals, with their white cross on the roof, are even spared in the bombing.

Both children, Paul and Ivan, are here in Presov, in an orphanage just a hundred feet away from me. It must be fairly cheerless there, but they will surely survive.

Perhaps the persecution will stop; no, this sort of thing won't stop just like that when it has only just started up again. But the Germans are just about to lose the war. It was clear to me that our world, the world in which we had grown up and been happy, had been destroyed, but if we were spared, we could begin again.

My mother is in Budapest, out of danger. My eldest sister, Eva, and her family are all in Switzerland. Magda, the second oldest, and the most belligerent of us sisters, had found shelter with her daughter, Susi, in the country. My youngest sister, Ilka, and her husband Miki, were alive and in a camp in Sered. I knew least about the fate of my husband's brothers and sisters. They had been deported to Poland. But perhaps they had been able to survive, I tried to hope for the best.

From time to time I fell asleep again. On her return home, Mrs Svaton brought me the news that the Gestapo had been back to the pharmacy several times to look for me. The next day flowed by in the same way, in an almost meditative peace, and I went over the situation again confidently. On the fourth day my feeling of security was shattered. Through the half-open window I heard the conversation between two neighbours. One said to the other in excited tones: "The Gestapo are looking for Mrs Lefkovits and her children". "Yes, I heard that too," answered the other indifferently. "The boys are in the orphanage in Jarkova Street, aren't they? They'll find them sooner or later." That went to my heart.

On the eighth day of my hard-to-bear concealment the air-raid sirens sounded again. In a terrible panic all the residents ran in fear to the air-raid shelter. The only one who didn't, although no less frightened than they were, was I. I stood under the arcade-like arch of the door, convinced that the bow in the thick old walls would withstand a bomb. The front of the house was razed to the ground, and some died too. Apart from fear and shock, nothing happened to me.

On that occasion Presov suffered massive bomb damage. Whole rows of houses lay shattered. After the all-clear I heard on the radio that the orphanage had also been hit. At that point no prohibition to go out, or the fact that it was getting dark, could hold me back. Muffled in a black headscarf and a dark coat borrowed from Katica, I ran like a mad woman to the orphanage. Thank God, I found my children there, safe and sound.

"We are evacuating the whole orphanage and everyone in it to the country," the Principal told me, and she offered to take little Ivan with them. However, we would have to find another hiding place for 14 year-old Paul. I couldn't bear the thought of separating the two boys. At that time I could never have imagined the dreadful, heartbreaking situation in which we did, after all, have to part.

A new solution for both children

As I left the orphanage, the situation seemed insoluble.

I went back to Katica's flat, but I was overcome with sadness. It was clear to me that I couldn't stay on with Katica. I could no longer take her willingness to sacrifice herself for granted, because from now on I represented an even greater danger to her. Perhaps someone had observed me in the house, or when I left her flat, or, who knows, was even now watching me come back, I worried en route.

Heavy with care, I went back inside. "The children are all right", was the first thing I said to her, noticing how she awaited my return with such sympathy. At the same time I told her what the Principal of the orphanage had said about evacuating the home, and she agreed with my decision not to separate the boys from each other. She thought that was correct and understandable.

As we had done a week before, we spent half the night thinking and planning. We considered how to find shelter for the children and where I could go. It seemed to us that the end of the war had crept even nearer. The sound of shell fire and grenades had grown louder and could be heard quite clearly. Perhaps when we awoke tomorrow morning the liberating Russian troops would already be here. . . so we thought. We must keep our nerve.

In the end Katica and I decided that she would go and inform Ivan's godfather, Josef Stracensky, in the morning and ask him for advice. Beaming with joy, she came back with an immediate response from Ivan's godfather. "He'll take both boys to the country with his own family". A stone fell from my heart.

At this point there is a large gap in my memory. Neither I, nor Ivan, can remember how they reached the little town of Lipovec (Szinye-Lipoc). Did they travel in a horse and cart, or by bus? Was it by day or night? Who fetched them from the orphanage? I only know that the two children arrived safe and sound in Lipovec.

A new haven was found for me by my dear good friend, Ilonka Friedmann-Mayer, who I will mention again frequently in my memoirs. I moved into the primitive ground-floor flat of Madame Elise, at number 111 Hinkova Street. That one and a half room flat already had four people living in it. I was the fifth.

A completely altruistic benefactress

Even in the most difficult and dangerous of times, there were people who put their own livelihood and even their lives on the line in order to save another human being. That was the case some time in March 1944, when our younger son, Ivan, who was then seven, was to be sent illegally to safety in Hungary.

The Jewish community in Hungary was still living in relative peace. The Nüremberg Laws did not yet apply to them, and, although they were not quite at ease, they were able to continue their careers without hindrance.

A young friend of ours, Mrs Olga R, managed with great difficulty to get hold of travel permits for a 14 year-old boy and a seven year-old girl. This had been organised by our wonderfully obliging friend, Dr Friedmann-Mayer, a paediatrician. Many Jewish children owe her their lives.

As I have already mentioned, one travel permit was for a seven year-old girl, the other for a 14 year-old boy. Our own little Ivan was, of course, a seven year-old boy, and the 14 year-old passenger, Vera Markus, was disguised as a boy. The preparations for the disguise and for the successful outcome of the venture for the children, were extremely nerve-wracking. At last the day of departure arrived. We were not able to accompany the travellers to the station, since the passes were for children whom we did not know. We learned the details about the journey from Presov much later from Mrs Olga R.

Well, they boarded the train and it left according to schedule. All seemed to be going smoothly. At the Slovakian/Hungarian border two border policemen came on board. They inspected all the documents, passes and suitcases in the normal way, found everything in order and left the compartment with a "have a good journey". Then followed an endlessly tense two or three hours of waiting before the Hungarian border and passport control police appeared. Mrs Olga and young Vera were shivering with apprehension when the two policemen came into their compartment. However, both men seemed to be very friendly, which dissipated the tense atmosphere.

"How old are you, little girl?" was the first question to little Ivan. "Seven", said the child proudly in Hungarian. "And what's your name?" came the second question from the official, who was continuing to examine the passport, leafing through from right to left.

"Well, uncle," said the child, slightly confused. "You see, till I get to the border my name is Jolan Varhal, and after the border my real name is Ivan Lefkovits." The policeman was completely taken aback. He sent his colleague into the next compartment to carry on with customs and passport control, presumably with the object of removing a witness to any further conversation.

He bent over the child and said in a very low and serious tone: "Do you know what would happen to all of you if I was a bad man? You would all three go straight to a concentration camp. Don't ever, anywhere, tell anyone what you have just told me. I didn't hear anything." Then he left the compartment.

Mrs Olga, who was nearly fainting with agitation, was hardly able to maintain her equilibrium. The 14 year-old girl was fighting tears, but knew that, as a boy, she mustn't cry. Little Ivan was blaming himself bitterly for his own stupidity and, sobbing, repeated over and over again, "Forgive me, forgive me."

The train moved off. Soon they were in Hungary, where ostensible freedom awaited them, but things were to turn out rather differently.

Mrs Olga R. had helped refugees before this journey and continued to do so afterwards, but she said that this journey to Budapest was probably the one that was the most nerve-wracking and, perhaps, the most dangerous.

Ivan in Budapest

When I think back to the the events of 1944, some of them seem clear, but some are hazy – like a badly-exposed film, where unimportant details appear more clearly than those in the foreground. Or still worse, it's like a photograph album which has fallen apart, where it is impossible to put the photographs back in to the right order.

I have a similar feeling about describing the story of Ivan's journey to Budapest, disguised in girl's clothing. Everything about that journey and subsequent events in Budapest was described to me afterwards by Mrs Olga R, and, very much later, by Ivan himself. Frau Olga handed the child over to the family of Dr Odon Propper. Ivan was very impressed by the city, but much more impressed by the many lovely toys that Dr Propper's son, who was quite a lot older than he was, possessed. Ivan was thrilled to be allowed to play with them.

The Propper family were distant relatives of ours, and Dr Propper had an established dental practice in Budapest. March 1944 was still a relatively peaceful time in Hungary. Their knowledge of the wave of persecution in Slovakia came only from the media. We had agreed with Dr Propper that Ivan could stay with them until all four of us, including my husband, the two children and myself, could meet up in Budapest as we planned. But our plan didn't work. Our attempt to cross the border into Hungary together failed. We made new plans to cross in two phases, but meanwhile my husband's health grew significantly worse – kidney failure. He finally reached Budapest with our friends, Mr and Mrs Samuel György, in a taxi on 12 March 1944. He was taken into the Jewish Hospital, and his very first visitor was Ivan. Paul and I were supposed to cross the 'green line' with the help of a 'person smuggler' on 20 March, and join my husband and Ivan. Just before we were due to leave, I received a telegram from Hungary by a roundabout route. It had no signature and just said "Don't come; stay where you are". At first I didn't understand it, until I heard on a neighbour's wireless (Jews were not allowed to own their own set) that the Germans had occupied Hungary.

The situation in Budapest changed dramatically from one day to the next. Dr Propper couldn't, or, perhaps, wouldn't look after my son any longer. Through his medical connections he managed to have little Ivan taken into an institution for deaf and dumb children. The decision to hide him there was taken from one hour to the next and there was no time to give him any instructions, other than to warn him briefly that "from now on, you mustn't say a single word". He was forced to adapt to the situation and in those comfortless surroundings had to learn sign language, all of which he did so quickly that he didn't even react to the howling air raid siren till his sleeve was plucked. I can't remember now how long he was there – four or five weeks? But sometimes, later on, even when he was once again able to speak aloud, he automatically used sign language.

The political situation had altered completely. It would have been pointless to escape to Hungary. Persecution and excess by the Slovak secret police and the Gestapo were the order of the day and deportation threw out its shadow. In independent Tiso-Slovakia a calmer period seemed to be beginning, so we had the children brought home. We no longer had a real 'home', since we had given up our house when we made the plans to flee to Hungary.

From one orphanage to another

I have strayed from the chronological order of my experiences in the previous chapters. Now I have reached the time (after Ivan's return from Budapest) where I had to look for new shelter for both children. I owe enormous thanks to Mrs Manci Skalny, who mobilised all her influence with the Catholic community in order to find a safe haven for my children. Both children were placed in a Catholic orphanage in Kremnica (Western Slovakia) under false names.

I received desperate letters from Paul, written at the Kremnica orphanage. The last one he sent from there ended with the words: "I don't want to be saved without you. I want the same thing to happen to me as to you. Ivan is too young to understand." The letter arrived by a roundabout route, since Jews were usually unable to receive post by conventional means. I don't need to describe the effect which that letter had on me. Around the beginning of September 1944 both boys appeared in Presov. Paul and his brother absconded from the orphanage, caught a night train, and, by changing trains several times and travelling by bus, they arrived back to where I was.

I was overcome with amazement. Of course I was delighted to have my children back with me, but this posed yet more problems. Where was I to house them? As I have mentioned before, we had given up our own home long ago. Since the failure of our plan to escape together to Hungary, I had been living with an old friend, Mrs Marta Blazek. Hesitantly, I asked her if I could have my children to live with me in my room.

I explained to her that the permit I held as a Jew with a 'reserved occupation' would act as a shield for Paul and Ivan. It would not be dangerous for her to shelter the children. She agreed without further ado and showed herself to be a good and true friend.

After I finished work at the pharmacy each day, I returned to my children. I listened with interest to the story of their experiences in Kremnica and their terrible journey (escape) to Presov.

My feelings of unease and worry grew all the time. A rumour was going round that some of the work permits issued by the authorities after the Slovak uprising might no longer be honoured by the Gestapo. With the help of our baptismal priest, Father Titus, we managed to get the children into the Presov orphanage.

When I was forced to leave the pharmacy so suddenly on 11 September, 1944, after Mrs Kissoczy's timely warning, I was comforted by the knowledge that the children were safe.

I should like to add a few words here about Father Titus. As soon as the persecution of the Jews started, people suggested that we should convert to Christianity and thus escape persecution. Father Titus performed this duty very uprightly and seriously and prepared us for this step over very many weeks. We were all baptised but, unfortunately, this was not enough to save us.

October 1944

So the children were in the care of the Presov orphanage. Since 11 September, I had been concealed by Katica Svaton, and so things continued until the mass bombing of Presov. The children were not evacuated with the rest of the orphanage because the Principal was only willing to take Ivan with them, but not Paul.

In this connection I remember Mr Josef Stracensky, a young, hard-working dental technician with great gratitude. His willingness to help manifested itself in the act of taking Paul and Ivan with him when he left Presov for Lipovec with his family. Any family that was able to avoid the air-raids, mainly aimed at the towns, escaped to the country at that time. Lipovec was a small, peaceful village near Presov, where the Stracensky family had a small flat.

I don't remember how long the children had been in Lipovec before I heard to my great surprise that they couldn't stay there any longer. What on earth had happened? What had happened was that my son, Paul, who was quite well-known as a good young footballer, had been recognised by a fellow player. "That's the son of Dr Lefkovits from Presov", shrieked one of them. Paul must not endanger the lives not only of the Stracensky family, but also the whole community, which might suffer by harbouring a Jewish child. There were two grounds for fearing this danger: first my family and I were already being hunted by the Gestapo, and secondly, persecution had increased enormously since the Slovak uprising.

There was nothing else for it. The two little ones would have to join me in my room at Madame Elise's, where there were already five of us.

I'll come back to that, but first I should like to tell you what happened later to the Stracensky family. Winter arrived. Even in Lipovec streams iced over. The village children played happily on the slides. Only the Stracensky family was unable to enjoy this winter. Their happy, healthy son had fallen over backwards on the slide and fractured his skull. They could not save him.

There was no comfort for this generous, God-fearing family for a long time. The saying "the Lord giveth and the Lord taketh away" for a long time brought them no peace. Mr Stracensky's great help was not the first good deed he had performed for us. His fate had been bound up with that of my husband for a very long time – in fact he had learned his trade from my husband. From 1928 onwards a father-son relationship had existed between the two of them. When he later joined the Hlinka Party, he used the influence and connections he gained from his membership to offer assistance whenever it was needed. And it was often needed.

Every time Hlinka Party members planned excesses against Jewish citizens, we were warned, but he could not always protect people from the nasty activities of the guardsmen. One day they happened to be searching for unlicensed weapons in my husband's practice. I was present during this house-search. As the men conducting the search opened the safe, one of them smuggled a loaded revolver into it. Triumphantly, he lifted this 'evidence' into the air, gloating to his accomplice: "Well, now we've found what we guessed was here". On the grounds of this false accusation, my husband was immediately arrested. He tried to defend himself by saying that he had had to hand over his rifle during the First World War, when he was wounded at the Front and taken prisoner by the Italians, and that he had not possessed any weapons since then, neither rifle nor revolver.

My innocent husband was released after Stracensky intervened, but this upset did a great deal of harm to his already fragile state of health.

Madame Elise

Counting my children, there were now seven people in hiding at the home of Madame Elise. For people from Presov who may read my memoirs, I should like to establish who was in this concealed group. They were: Desider Weiszhaus, an engineer, his wife Ilonka, nee Grün, their son Jani, me and my two children, and Klari Fischer, Dr Friedmann-Mayer's niece.

A bit later an eighth person was added – none of us knew his identity. We called him Walter, and from the little he said we gathered only that, after many blows from fate and much suffering, he had escaped in Rumania while being transported.

The windows of our flat opened on to Jarkova Street. Thick curtains prevented anyone seeing in or out, the light was never switched on and the darkened windows were never opened. Our hostess, Madame Elise, was a hairdresser in peacetime, and lived in this primitive, old-fashioned flat with her sick and elderly mother. She did not charge an exorbitant price for supplying us with a hiding-place and food, but poor Madame Elise placed herself in great danger, for which money could not compensate her, and she paid with her life. When they arrested us, the Gestapo did not spare her. She was deported along with us, and in the thin clothing she was given to replace the winter clothes brought from home, she was unable to withstand the biting cold and frost. Within a week at Ravensbrück she was dead.

Now events are out of sequence again. I want to tell you how they came to find us in our hiding-place. It happened like this:

We were concealed in a dark, windowless space, like an ante-room. A very steep and narrow wooden staircase led from the floor of this room into a huge, deep cellar. The entrance to the top of the staircase was shut off by a heavy divided trap-door, which was covered by a strong, heavy carpet. No-one would be able to guess what was hidden by that carpet.

A good-natured old neighbour prepared our food. She did it out of pure kindness of heart, but she was certainly putting her own life on the line. With the agreement of the Slovak authorities, the Germans were offering a reward of five hundred crowns to anyone who could put them on the trail of where and with whom any Jews might be hidden. Concealment was punishable by death.

It was no easy task to produce nourishment for so many people without attracting attention. But Mrs T did it for weeks on end. Each evening she brought food to us in our hiding-place.

The three children, three lively boys, found their incarceration very hard. They were not allowed to talk loudly, had to move about the room very softly (because the floorboards creaked) and behave quietly. It was late autumn. The days were drawing in and we were not permitted to switch on the lamp or light a candle. An extremely depressing situation. But our survival depended on our retaining our zest for living.

The Front was getting nearer (Presov is not far from the Polish border). The rapid advance of the Red Army and the frequent very loud sound of shells being fired gave us comfort and the hope that it couldn't last for much longer.

It must have been around 22 November when Madame Elise burst into our room, fear and trepidation in her face. "The Gestapo are searching the house", she stuttered, deathly pale with anxiety. "Quickly. Into the cellar". In seconds we had tidied away the few possessions which would have betrayed the fact that someone was living there. In great haste, Madame Elise lifted away the carpet that covered the opening. Like a wild lion, Walter threw up the great trapdoor and we ran down like hunted beasts. I pulled my children close to me, and we waited in great anxiety to discover what was going on above our heads.

The heavy threatening footsteps of the searchers had faded away. Silence fell. Madame Elise pulled the carpet away from the trapdoor and Walter opened it. With a feeling of great relief we climbed out of the cellar. From the pale, exhausted appearance of the landlady, we could see that the search had not gone completely smoothly.

At the time we could not know that we had made one fateful mistake – little Ivan's slipper had fallen off his foot in the hasty descent to the cellar. None of us noticed it, but, in any case, there would have been no time to pick it up. The guard found it and in a deep and threatening voice asked what it was. Quick as a flash Madame Elise kept her presence of mind and, almost laughing, said: "My cat likes to play with that. I've been looking for it for ages. I'm so glad you have found it." Two or three days passed in apparent peace. We continued to think that no-one was aware of our existence, apart from our landlady and Mrs T.

One frosty winter's night the guard (a member of the local fascist Hlinka Garde) came back, accompanied by two Gestapo men. They found us asleep in our beds, so he had obviously not believed the fairy story about the cat and had passed on his suspicions to his superiors. And that is how they were able to catch another eight people.

If Walter had had better luck, there would only have been seven. He was hiding under the bed, but they found him just the same (the Gestapo knew there should be eight of us anyway) and he was badly beaten.

November 1944

When we climbed down from the lorry at the prison gate, we and our meagre possessions were ordered into an ice-cold room. The wave of arrests must have been highly successful, since a great many Jewish families had already been delivered there from their hiding-places. Among others in that huge room I recognised the Engländer sisters and Mr and Mrs Altmann.

I was taken for interrogation like the others. I had been expecting the questions – how long had we been in hiding, where was my husband, and where might others be concealed – so I was able to avoid incriminating anyone else. Unprepared and bewildered, I heard them pass the verdict that helping the partisans had cost us dear. Had somebody betrayed us?, I mused afterwards. Would non-Jewish employees from the pharmacy be arrested too? I and a few others were ordered to clear snow. We had hardly started with the spades, when one of the guards told me to stop shovelling and to follow him. On the way he informed me urgently, but confidentially, that I and my children could be spared a great deal of unpleasantness, abasement and beating in the next few difficult days, if I were to give him all my money and valuables. He pointed out that they would be taken from me anyway, so I gave him everything I had with me.

After the war I saw him once more, but I'll tell you about that later.

Deportation from Presov

On 26 November, 1944, we were herded into freezing cattle trucks standing in a siding at Presov Station. Loading the cattle trucks is perhaps the one activity which it would be superfluous to describe. Such scenes are familiar enough. "Los! Los!", blows with rifle-butts for those who falter, and the humiliation of the persecuted were caught on celluloid by many amateur and professional photographers.

We were hauled from prison late at night. The citizens of the town had gone to bed long before. This last transport was supposed to take place in complete secrecy. On the transport there were doctors, pharmacists, medical personnel and people who, until a month ago, had been Jews in 'reserved occupations'. Their exceptional status and work permits had been withdrawn from them. They were arrested and given one hour in which to pack a few necessities. With true German precision, a list was drawn up with names, dates of birth and occupations, and when the right number of prisoners was reached, they were delivered to the station for transportation.

We were told we would have to work in different places in Germany, where our labour, partly for the civil authorities and partly for the war effort, was urgently needed. We didn't believe a word of it; even Dr and Mrs Duschnitz didn't believe it.

Dr Duschnitz was a respected, much-loved old doctor, whose wife, a former opera singer from Vienna, came from a highly-cultured old German family. As the oldest, and last, Jewish doctor in Presov, he still had permission to treat Jewish patients. He was even allowed to employ 'Aryan' staff. On 25 November, 1944, two Gestapo men rang his doorbell. As befitted this cultured couple, the two polite young men were received courteously and invited to take a seat. The two Gestapo men conversed for a little while with the couple, who spoke faultless German, then an embarrassed silence ensued. The two men got to their feet and said politely: "It's not what we want, but we have orders from above. In your own interests and for your own safety, we have to arrest you."

Dr Duschnitz knew it would be hopeless to protest, but he

begged the two men for a couple of hours' delay, so that they could pack a few necessities. The Gestapo men agreed and left the house. When they came back they found the bodies of the couple. So Dr and Mrs Duschnitz were spared the dreadful suffering and degradation that would have been their lot.

There was something exceptional and special about this couple. As if they knew from the beginning what would happen to them, and to all of us. They had even ordered their gravestone right at the start of the Nazi persecution, and had it engraved with their names and dates of birth. After the war, the Jewish community had the task of adding the date of their death. The admiration I have felt for this couple all these years has never slackened.

On the way to destruction

We were squashed together in the freezing cattle-truck. Those near the side were frozen after a quarter of an hour; those in the middle were warm, but had nothing to hold on to. As if petrified, we stood leaning against one another for a while, then the doors were sealed.

We didn't know how long this journey would last, whether hours or days, until we would be freed from this unbearable situation. Little groups formed. Families, friends, acquaintances moved close together wherever possible, to lean on each other, support or hold on to each other.

Slowly the train rolled into motion. The narrow slits of the air-vents let in a dim light and the biting cold. We had long ago lost our watches, so that we could follow the passage of time only by our growing hunger and even greater thirst.

The train moved slowly, stopped often in open country and in the sidings of various small stations. Secretly, we hoped we would not leave Slovakia, or the area of the old Czechoslovakia. I recollect vividly the first stop, when they unsealed the door and let us or forced us out. There was a field kitchen nearby, and the smell arising from it floated over to us. At that station we were given some sort of warm liquid, perhaps a root broth, and at last a drink of water. We were not allowed to stray far from the wagons. "Los! Los! Einsteigen!", and the journey continued. It was hard to keep track of the number of days and nights.

"Did you see them add on even more trucks? This is an enormous scrap collection, this transport; there must be at least 700 people", said one young man. "Nonsense, there are exactly 1,000 souls", said another. "I used to see the documents when I worked in the office. They deport 1,000 people on every transport. If for any reason they don't reach the correct total, they fill the transport with people who are intended for a different one." We ought to have had supplies for at least three days, but this transport was different. It consisted mainly of people who had been arrested at night or during snap arrests.

"I know for certain", continued the man, "that in every truck there is a Jewish orderly with a white band on his right arm, who is responsible for order on the train. On other transports a Jewish doctor would be assigned, with responsibility for the health of those being deported."

On our transport, that precaution would be superfluous, since nearly every one of us was either a doctor, a pharmacist or a member of the medical profession.

The man appeared to be well-informed. "There are a medicine-chest and two stretchers in each truck. The commandant of the transport hands over a list of deportees to the German authorities at the German border, and the medicine-chest, the stretchers and the bucket go back to Slovakia. The doors must be kept closed while on Slovak territory."

How Walter had prepared and carried out his escape under such strict conditions, we could not fathom. We, who had been squashed up against each other in the truck, had been unaware of any noise which would have alerted us to the work of a saw, chisel, drill or screwdriver. Or had the groans of the old and the sobs of the young drowned out the noise? When we climbed out of the cattle-truck, Walter was no longer there. A square opening appeared to have been cut out of the floor. When and where he had escaped, we never discovered, and we don't know whether or not he survived. If anyone who reads my book recognises the brave man who shared our hiding-place from this description, I would be most grateful to hear about his fate.

When, at last, the train stopped, seventeen corpses were un-loaded from our wagon. I don't know how many there were in the other ones.

Nearly fifty years have gone by since that time. I am still amazed today how much we were able to endure. Did these terrible events really happen?

After we left the train, we waited patiently for the lavatory. The queue moved forwards very slowly. I looked for another way in and opened an unlabelled door. On the operating table I caught sight of bloody human remains. Nearly fainting, I rejoined my group and said nothing to anyone about it.

We had reached Ravensbrück.

Ravensbrück

The surroundings, the barbed wire and the watchtowers were just as alarming for me as the inscription in huge lettering: "ARBEIT MACHT FREI".

All the men and boys over 14 were separated from us and taken away to the men's camp. At that moment I was struck with the most inconsolable grief, for my 14 year-old, my little Paul, went with the men. Dreadful pain and terrible hopelessness gripped me. I held Ivan's hand and stood as if turned to stone. There I was, parted from my husband, lying desperately ill thousands of kilometres away in the Budapest Jewish Hospital, and now I was separated from Paul by the implacable barbed wire. . . I can hardly describe my desperation at these partings.

Ivan and I remained together in the 'Mother and Child' hut, barrack number 12. The first news I had about Paul came on a greasy bit of paper which my good friend, Dr Bela Rosenberg, sent to me from the men's camp. "Zsuzsa, don't worry about Paul. We will look after him."

I kept that greasy piece of paper with me all the time, and when my despair grew unbearable, I took it out and read it a hundred times, to keep up my strength in case of worse to come. I have always thought of Dr Rosenberg with gratitude and mentioned him in my prayers.

Early in the morning and evening we were given a lukewarm brown liquid, coffee substitute, which contained some kind of sedative, probably bromide. We received our bread ration in the morning, and tried somehow to make it last all day. There was nowhere to put it down or keep it, but it was important to keep something to eat in the evening. The only warm meal was soup, which was given to us in the evening. One way to improve the 'menu' was to volunteer to work outside. I did that often, and that way I think I managed to ensure that Ivan had at least a minimal intake of calories.

From one day to the next we became ugly, unkempt, apathetic beings, dressed in rags. Although they did not cut off our hair, we looked so awful that, when we met while washing, we hardly recognised each other. The washing facilities consisted of a grey cement trough fixed along the wall. Anyone wanting to wash had to find space at the trough. Fourteen or fifteen women at a time were squashed into the washroom, and we hardly had time for the most primitive cleansing, before we were herded out and the tap turned off.

Hygienic conditions were indescribable. Diarrhoea posed great danger for everyone. Not only did it weaken the body, but it was also sometimes impossible to wash one's hands afterwards. The stink was overlaid with that of chloride of lime, and even today I still have the penetrating smell in my nostrils.

If we were able to empty our bowels each evening and crawl into our bunks with clean hands afterwards, we felt we were still members of the human race.

Roll-call was at five in the morning and usually lasted for four to four and a half hours. But if someone was late or didn't appear at all, everyone was punished by having to stand in the freezing cold for an extra two hours. We had very little on, since we had been given summer dresses to wear instead of the good warm clothing we had brought. with us from home. Through indifference and sheer cruelty the dresses were doled out regardless of body size. In fact it appeared that small delicate women were given the biggest clothes, and large, fat women the mini-sizes on purpose. The same happened with shoes. Very few prisoners had the chance to get hold of anything warmer. For example, I survived the endless freezing roll-call clad in a thin georgette dress and a light coat.

A few days after we arrived, we received typhoid innoculations. The injections were terribly painful. The needles on the syringes had become completely blunted, but they used the same syringe again and again. Many of the doses received were far too large, and most people had a reaction with high fever and terrible pain in the whole of their back.

After roll-call, I was detailed to a labour group whose job it was to carry five or six-metre long telegraph poles between two of us on our shoulders from one place to another. After the third circuit I realised that I wasn't going to survive this situation very long. The pain was getting worse and I had a high temperature. I guessed I couldn't hold out for much longer. All of a sudden, with my brow dripping with sweat, I knew I would collapse after twenty more steps.

The girl dragging the poles along with me was a strong young Hungarian, not yet worn out by the work, who had had her inoculation much earlier. I could see that she had drawn the short straw today and was going to die because of me. I didn't want simply to collapse under the heavy burden, and so, quite exhausted, I said to her: "Juliska, I'm going to put the pole down." "Dear God, please don't do that", she begged me. "They'll shoot us on the spot."

At that moment an overseer went by. "Excuse me, Herr Oberscharführer," I sobbed. "I can't go on. I'm sick." And I lowered the pole from my shoulder. He looked at me and asked me what I had done for a living in civilian life. "I was a pharmacist", I replied. "Leave it there", he said and continued on his way. His behaviour seemed miraculous, and for a moment we stood transfixed, until we realised we were not going to be shot. We could not decide whether to stay there or move on. Since we received no further orders, we made our way slowly to the assembly point.

On the way Juliska told me that she had been deported from Budapest just a few weeks earlier. I was very surprised to hear that transports were still arriving from Budapest. She explained to me that, since the German occupation, the 'American Safe House', where countless Jewish citizens in possession of US travel documents had found shelter, was no longer recognised as such by the Nyilas fascist organisation and Gestapo. With the exception of elderly people, all its occupants had been deported. In great agitation I asked whose American documents were still valid. When I pressed her, she could only remember one name: "Mrs Anna Strauss". "Oh dear God!", I cried in excitement and joy. "That's my mother."

A small ray of hope, that my darling mother would survive persecution in Budapest, arose in me. It was not until I went home after the war, following the Liberation, that I learned about my poor mother's unhappy fate and demise from people returning from Budapest.

The death of my mother

When the Allies bombed Budapest in Spring 1945, my mother could not get down into the air-raid shelter. She stayed upstairs on the third floor of the house and heard the thunder of the approaching bomb drops. She could tell from the vibration that this time the bombers were aiming straight for the house where she was, and that is exactly what happened. The building sustained a direct hit, the walls fell in, the house collapsed inwards, and only the outer walls and one corner arch remained standing. As if protected by God's will, my mother survived unscathed in that corner of the ruined room.

She was rescued from the third floor by firemen with ladders, and brought to safety. Many residents who had sought refuge in the shelters died in the ruins.

After the air-raids, and presumably as a direct result of them, there was a typhoid epidemic in Budapest. Having survived the bombing, my mother was unable to fight the illness. The shock to her system had brought her so low that she had no more resistance. My poor mother died at the age of 77.

She was spared the dreadful sorrow that the loss of so many of her relatives would have caused. She did not have her own grave, nor a headstone, but was buried in a mass grave in the Kerepesi cemetary in Budapest. Decades later my sister Ilka and I could do no more than lay a wreath of flowers next to the memorial plaque.

Without exception, every member of my family who was killed ended up in a mass grave. On my mother's side, everyone in the family who had not been taken in the main wave of deportations in 1942, because they were doctors, pharmacists, etc., was killed by the Germans, together with hundreds of others, after the Slovak uprising in 1944. They were lined up (near Kremnica) and shot into their grave. Among them was a small, seven year old piano virtuoso called Katica Fésüs who, so it was prophesied, should have had a glittering musical future ahead of her.

We didn't believe it

When they showed the film 'Holocaust' on TV in 1982, my then 18 year-old grandson asked me in shock and agitation: "Granny, why didn't you fight back at all, at least like the Poles in the Warsaw Ghetto? Why did you let yourselves be taken like lambs to the slaughter without saying a word?"

It was difficult to answer that question. Anyone who was not there and did not know what things were like then, cannot understand. Embarrassed, I tried to make our 'cowardice' comprehensible through various attempts at explanation. Not everybody can be a fighter, and we didn't go to our death through cowardice, but we found out very quickly that resistance to the machinery of mass murder would be useless.

We were too slow to recognise the danger, and once we did, it was already too late. When Czechoslovakia was founded, the large Jewish minority was already very heterogeneous and stratified. They had become more and more assimilated during the twenty years of democratic development and we deluded ourselves that we were esteemed Czechoslovak citizens, who would not be left in the lurch.

We knew what was going on in Germany, and were alarmed by it. But when we saw that many persecuted German Jews came to us in safe Czechoslovakia for refuge, we imagined we must be secure. After the Germans occupied the Czech part of the Czechoslovak Republic, i.e. Bohemia and Moravia, and an independent Slovakia, with a priest as head of state, was formed out of the Slovak part in 1939 with German blessing, we buried our worries about the unthinkable.

We just could not comprehend that our husbands, brothers, sons, who had built up and worked with the state, would be let down by the community and mercilessly driven to death from overwork and starvation. And we just could not believe that the life of a young girl, deported in her prime in 1942, might hang on a simple hand-movement from Mengele – "to the right" or "to the left".

A few might have been able to and did save themselves. Other families, like ours, stayed on, and our fate was sealed. Our greatest error was our lack of willingness to give up our high standard of living, our lifestyle, our position in the world of work and politics. In addition, we didn't leave our lovely homes soon enough. We were convinced that persecution could not lead to deportation. The old people and those in essential occupations (doctors, pharmacists, etc.), who had been spared in the first wave of deportations, encouraged each other to think that we only needed to keep our nerve and our loved ones would soon be home again.

I had plenty of time to reproach myself for all the things I could or should have done or not done, but since then I have become convinced that, although it was possible for individuals to be saved, there was no possibility of rescue for the Jews as a whole. There was only one opportunity to die upright and with pride, and they did that in the Warsaw Ghetto. They did it for all those of us whose self-respect as human beings had been torn from them.

We did everything we could to help our relatives and friends who had been deported to Poland. We paid Polish couriers, who could cross the border without difficulty, so that they would secretly provide valuables,food and clothing for the deportees. We never found out whether they received any of it, some of it or none of it, since nothing was ever recorded on paper.

Readers of these lines, who were acquainted with circumstances in Presov, will know who Mrs Anna Rosenberg was. She ran the 'Jewish Womens' Group' and her husband, Dr Theophil Rosenberg, was chairman of law chambers in Presov. Her wonderful charitable work was known everywhere and she helped Jews and non-Jews, wherever she could.

However, even she could not escape a tragic fate. As they loaded the last of the sick and elderly on to the cattle trucks for transportation, she suddenly began to search impatiently for something in her handbag, took out a tiny note and went hurriedly up to the official from the 'Central Organisation for Jews', who was overseeing the departure of the wagons.

"Mr B, would you be so kind as to give this note to my housekeeper, so that she can collect the starched collars and cuffs from the cleaners, ready for us to have on our return?"

It had never crossed Mr and Mrs Rosenberg's minds that they might never need starched collars and cuffs again.

Aussenkommando

I still have very vivid memories not only of carrying the heavy poles, but also all the other things I had to do on this outside duty. The exclusive aim of this work was to weaken the prisoners enough to kill them off sooner. As I have already mentioned, it was possible to volunteer for this duty. The reward was an extra bowl of soup, but that wasn't always the case. Often prisoners on outside duty remained out there – beaten or shot. I took that risk – the extra bowl of soup for Ivan was worth it for me.

The duty consisted of us pushing a wheelbarrow laden with newly dug earth to a distant spot somewhere, emptying it out, pushing the empty barrow back from whence we had come, filling it up once more and emptying it out again on to the growing heap. Since we were poorly nourished and scantily clad, it was only a question of time before we collapsed from exhaustion. Only a few were able to hold out.

Two merciless women overseers had the job of supervising the intermittent work of the prisoners. They were accompanied by two superbly trained German Shepherd dogs, who were so amazingly well drilled that, if anyone remained standing or stopped work for too long, the two furious dogs would leap barking shrilly on to the 'striking' women and tear the clothes from their backs.

Filled with dreadful fear and terror, the women would move off again. The overseers fell about laughing, and the dogs knew they had done their duty. They immediately stopped tearing the clothing and returned to their 'mistresses'.

Since then I have never been able to look at a German Shepherd dog without fear and trembling.

December 1944

Ravensbrück was actually a women's camp, but from 1944 onwards they provided a few huts for 'mothers and children'. We were allocated a place in one of those huts. There was no way of knowing how many mothers and children spent their imprisonment there, since some died every day. Despairing and helpless we were forced to listen to the sobbing supplications of our dying children: "Mummy, I'm hungry; I'm very hungry". "Please, please, darling Mummy, I want some water!" But none of the 'Mummies' could help. If all the crying and begging disturbed the overseer in the next room, she would shout harshly: "Be quiet, or I'll throw you all out". But there was no silence until the dying children had no strength left to beg for food or drink, but fell asleep – for ever. The only reason why mothers who found the half-frozen corpses of their beloved children by their side did not go mad with pain, destroy everything and hit the overseer in the face with their fists, must have been that our coffee was laced with bromide or other sedatives.

Even my own Ivan fell ill. He had a high temperature and unbearable pain in his head and ears. I took him to the sick-bay, where a young Belgian doctor with a purple triangle on her overall, diagnosed middle ear infection in both ears. The only thing she had to give him was a bit of substitute aspirin, and she left us with the sound advice that we should make Ivan a poultice. In her opinion, it would be better if he did not survive the illness, since he would probably be completely deaf in both ears afterwards.

I didn't volunteer to work outside after that, and I was not ordered to go either. I had to appear at roll-call with Ivan, and he leaned against me with a high temperature. The worst times were at night, when my son asked me for something, and could not hear my answers. He cried bitterly and said over and over again: "Mummy, I've got such a terrible headache and my ears hurt such a lot. I keep on talking to you and you don't answer me." I clutched him close to me, so that at least he could feel that I was right next to him.

After a few days in agony, first one ear, then the other, opened up of their own accord. Presumably Nature, and the hot poultices, did the trick. I made them by soaking a cloth with hot coffee. Luckily the Belgian doctor was wrong. Ivan's hearing in both ears is unimpaired .

When we first arrived in Ravensbrück, we were given a daily portion of bread, coffee substitute and soup. Occasionally, we received a portion of margarine. At Christmas, 1944, we were even amazed to have the chance to enjoy a piece of sausage.

January 1945

We had already been in Ravensbrück for more than two months. During that time many friends and relatives from the Presov transport had died. It was hard to comprehend why the strongest and healthiest people, and those who were still fairly young, seemed to be the least able to withstand the bodily and spiritual degradation. They were the first to die.

One of our 'Aryan' friends, Maria Boros, who had been sent to camp because she was married to a Jew, had died by the end of her second week, despite her previously excellent health and sportive lifestyle.

Dr Müller's wife, who had been renowned for her beauty in Presov, suffered a tragic fate. She had false 'Aryan' papers and was living in the High Tatras, at the Sonntagh Sanatorium. At a party there, a German Nazi-party member recognized her, saying: "I know her from Presov. She's not an Aryan." She was deported next day and was in the same hut as we were. She did not survive.

At Ravensbrück there were three generations of prisoners in some families. Mrs Serene Sommer, her daughter, Marta and her grandson, Zsigi, were all on our transport to Ravensbrück – or was it the one before? I met Serene in the sick-bay, where she was in a bad way. Some weeks later, after our transfer to Bergen-Belsen concentration camp, Marta and Zsigi were in the same block as we were. By that time Serene was dead. I will come back to that later, mainly to mention Zsigi, who was the same age as Ivan. He was the only one of his family who survived the hell we went through, and he now lives in Switzerland and has remained one of our best friends.

Ivan was eight on 21 January, and I had my birthday on 25 January – sad birthdays for both of us.

February 1945

We were getting weaker and weaker, and our 'life' was becoming much worse – even more unbearable and completely without hope. But we had a view over the whole block and gradually got to know who everybody was. We knew who was next to us and who lay above us, and we also knew who was alive and who had died. One morning, after roll-call, we were transferred. No-one told us why and we didn't guess the reason. Anyway, we ended up in a different block. This hut had no bunks, only long rows of straw-filled sacks, and this was where we were to live from now onwards. The babble of languages was even greater here – a complete tower of Babel. The inmates of two or perhaps three blocks had been transferred to this one, that is to say, the survivors from them, since many many people had died. Apart from German, one heard all the Slav languages, and also Hungarian, Italian, French, Dutch and Flemish. In our block, the most common language in use was Ukrainian.

The Italians found the raw climate hardest to endure. I met a young teacher from Padua. She had just arrived, and I was already an experienced prisoner at the time. I warned her to lay every stitch of clothing that she was not wearing under her head at night, and to tie her bundle with any remaining bits of bread in it to her wrist. Nocturnal stealing took place day in day out, and was getting worse and worse from week to week. At dusk gangs of women set off. There were only three or four of these groups, mostly twos or threes, searching for their victims. They gagged their mouths so that they could not call for help, tied them up and robbed them of everything. These primitive women, stripped of all human qualities by hunger, would kill for a piece of bread.

Despite my warning, the delicate Italian woman could not escape an assault. She was robbed of all her 'worldly goods'. This time it wasn't just her bread ration, but her missing coat that was her downfall. In the morning she had to stand for hours in the freezing cold at roll-call, with no warm clothing on, started a high fever, and, three days later, was dead.

Something similar nearly happened to me, but I was able to avert it. It was still quite early in the night; my fellow prisoners were not yet asleep but just resting their weary bodies ready for morning roll-call. Suddenly I noticed that three shadowy figures were approaching my bed in the gloom and aiming to tear off the bundle tied to my wrist. But before they could get a hold on me, I shouted at the top of my voice: "Help, help! I'm in danger; I'm being attacked".

Those of my fellow countrywomen who still had the strength to do so, came over from the other end of the sleeping area to protect me. In my linen bundle I kept not bread, as my assailants thought, but Ivan's little felt boots, which we had brought with us from home.

The gang of women retreated, perhaps to seek out another victim.

Last days in Ravensbrück

We were completely isolated from the outside world and had no idea what was going on out there. From time to time news came by word of mouth from the men's camp, which was supposed to imbue us with courage.

Once an old soldier risked his own life to bring us a note on which was written: "Hold out! Don't despair. It's nearly over – we will survive!"

This little letter worked miracles. In our thoughts we had already gone home. We made plans about what we would do once we were free! What would be the very first thing we would cook or bake? We were already swapping recipes, while our stomachs were still rumbling with hunger.

Our optimism dwindled. Day by day more and more corpses were being fetched out of the block. The bread rations grew smaller, the soup thinner and less palatable. There was no longer any sign of sausage. Previously, if anyone did not appear punctually for roll-call, or was even absent, everybody was punished by an extra roll-call and the guilty received extra punishment, frequently being beaten to death.

This stopped now. Quite a few overseers and 'trusties' were transferred, though we didn't know the rhyme or reason for this. Had they been too strict? Or were they beginning to have doubts about the future of the thousand-year empire, and suddenly treating their unhappy prisoners with a little more humanity?

We could hear the many aeroplanes flying overhead and the nightly air-raids. Air-raid warnings were the order of the day, but they didn't affect us, since the only shelter was for the soldiers, the SS and the camp administrators. There was no need to protect prisoners from the bombing, if they were condemned to death anyway. But the Allies seemed to know the location of the concentration camps, or at least where ours was, and we did not suffer any bomb damage.

March 1945

During the first half of March we heard murmurings that we were to evacuate the camp. We couldn't imagine how this was to be achieved. What were their plans? Would it be a genuine evacuation, or just mass murder? Where would they take us? In which direction? Still further away from home? Would we be herded into cattle trucks, or transported in lorries? Prisoners returning from duty outside the camp reported that many roads had been bombed and were impassable.

However, the answer, when it came, was even more gruesome for our block. We were to walk! It was to be a week-long 'death march'. My little Ivan, already weakened by the effects of a poor diet and his double middle-ear infection, couldn't hold out for long. Apart from that, he had problems with his boots, which had become much too tight for him, cramping his toes and bending them further and further in.

I carried him on my back for a bit, then he dragged himself along for a bit. Then I would pick him up again, but I couldn't do it for long. Even today I look back with eternal thanks to Klari Fischer, who was with us on this death march – she survived. She took it in turns with me to carry Ivan on our backs. Innumerable bodies of exhausted or dead women lay at the side of the road, some shot. Gradually we threw away most of our pathetic possessions to lighten the load and survive the march. In our little knapsacks we anxiously hoarded little bits of clothing which we had rescued from dead companions in suffering.

We stopped for the night in barns on small-holdings. We were even better pleased if there was a stable, because the animals provided us with a bit of warmth. Occasionally we met generous people, mostly elderly, who watched us in anguish. In one barn an old lady brought us bread and warm milk, which she had hidden in a small basket. We just couldn't believe it – milk and soft bread! This meant an awful lot to us, not only for our rumbling stomachs, but also for our spirits, as a gesture giving us hope that we might survive. The few hours we spent on the soft straw seemed to us like a short dream. However, before long, the merciless SS man would shout:

"Los! Los! Weiter! Rasch!", and we would be herded further along our dangerous, futureless road.

But some people could not get up from the straw. Bodies were left behind in every barn and all the time fewer and fewer of us were capable of walking any further. Days passed, nights flew by. Did it last seven days?

Suffering dreadfully, we reached Bergen-Belsen.

Fifty years have passed since then, but this is the first time that I have tried to write about the indescribable suffering and awful pain. There were two reasons for not writing. "Time heals wounds", they say, but even after fifty years these wounds remain unhealed, even if they are hidden below the surface. And I also worry that readers will make comparisons between my own story and Nazi atrocities in general, saying: "well, at least *she* got warm milk and bread". I am not a believer in collective guilt, but just because a few people did show a little human kindness, I cannot forgive all the guilty ones. I might be able to do so for myself, but not on behalf of the millions who died in misery. However, if I don't tell my story in the evening of my years, who will?

I was never religious, but had always believed in God. But how can anyone continue to believe in God when He manifestly allowed such terrible atrocities to happen?

Arrival in Bergen-Belsen

At long last we arrived at Bergen-Belsen, in indescribably dire distress and misery. We had to form up in front of a long wooden house and stand there for hours. We were shivering with fatigue, cold and hunger in the sharp north wind. We were on the same latitude as Hanover, and it was freezing cold.

They told us we would be able to have a bath, but couldn't imagine that we would ever get clean again. The only thing we could see was that every so often a group of fifteen to twenty completely exhausted women and a few children from among the ones who had survived the death march, would be let into the wooden building. We never saw anyone come out.

"They must be gas chambers", we whispered to each other despairingly. "But why bring us all the way from Ravensbrück, just to execute us here?", we tried to comfort ourselves.

They weren't gas chambers. Later on we learned that Bergen-Belsen didn't have any gas chambers. In this camp exhausted prisoners died of hunger and cruel treatment.

Little Ivan couldn't stand up any more, and slowly sank to my feet. He waited in apathetic despair till our turn came. At last an enormous door opened and we could feel the warm air streaming out of it. Quite calmly we obeyed the brusque order to throw all our clothes on to a pile. "Los! Los!", shrieked the SS men once again, herding us naked into another room. Hot water streamed from the ceiling and we washed ourselves. We had lost any fear of gas and just wanted to enjoy the healing warmth, while rinsing off all the dirt and filth.

At the other end of the room they opened an immense folding door and pushed us out from under the hot showers into the icy March chill. On a table outside lay a pile of disinfected clothing, which we hurriedly put on over our wet bodies, for that chill was just another form of murder.

In my mind I remember the sequence of events exactly, but there are some circumstances which do need clarifying. I refer you to the chapter at the end 'How accurate is this book?' – so that I don't have to leave my story here.

In Belsen without hope

There were huts for 'mothers and children' here too, and Ivan and I ended up in one. Our new quarters were full, much more crowded than in Ravensbrück, but everyone just had to squeeze closer together after our arrival. We met many friends and acquaintances there, including the wife of Dr Grosswirth-Weiner and her two daughters, and Mrs Sari Brody and her child. Mrs Marta Baumöhl and her small son, Zsigi, were next to us and we lay with our heads close together.

Despite being so crowded and overflowing, it seemed to be quite tidy, if one can use such an expression here. Our first walk to the huts after the shower episode, had actually given us a much worse impression. To left and right we saw bodies. We were used to seeing dead people in Ravensbrück – people who had been shot or who had chosen the barbed wire as a release – but these bodies were different.

These bodies were not those of half-starved prisoners, but skeletons, revealed through pathetic bits of clothing. What hunger, sorrow and agony had they suffered?

Our most urgent concern was to get something to eat, and we were given some bread and a portion of soup. Our new existence had begun. In the morning we were amazed to find that we wouldn't have to attend roll-call. "We don't have roll-call", said a Mrs G from Brünn, and the rest of her sentence was filled with irony. "This is a rest-camp, not a work-camp". Our first trip outside the hut was to the latrines. There were toilets in our block, but you had to queue up.

As the days went on we had to squeeze up closer and closer, as more transports arrived. The growing piles of corpses made room for the newcomers.

Water was in ever shorter supply, cases of dysentery multiplied and a typhoid epidemic broke out. A third disease, tuberculosis, began to spread. We could distinguish between the diseases and their symptoms. Diarrhoea, headaches, cramps, breathing difficulties, coughing up blood, were all not just something we were aware of around us, but involved us directly.

We hardly ever saw any SS men or women, and Mrs G told us why, but warned us at the same time: "They know they have lost, but they don't want to leave any witnesses behind. They'll just leave us to die like animals; nobody will survive this."

I had heard enough. Every day I could see people getting more and more apathetic, but I must be strong. Mrs G continued: "Have you heard of Josef Kramer? No? Nor Irma Grese? No? Well, Josef Kramer is the commandant of this camp, a brutal chap. They even say he is proud of his nickname, the Beast of Belsen. But the true Beast is Irma Grese, who has the face of an angel and a whip. She is still all-powerful here, and she does still patrol. If you see her, look away and keep out of sight till she has gone past."

Our conditions deteriorated very quickly. Occasionally we were given soup, but it was not always accompanied by bread. People were always on the look-out for something to steal, so I didn't dare leave Ivan alone and thieving was something I was not able to learn how to do. We scrounged a little here, a little there, and sometimes even shared in the proceeds of theft. The 'successful' ones gobbled anything edible – if they could find it. It was impossible to store anything, and even the thieves had things stolen from them.

We realised the important fact that it took very little to satisfy our hunger. Our stomachs seemed to have shrunk, so that we needed much less food. It worried me very much to see that Ivan was developing the symptoms of much feared oedema in the legs and stomach.

It was rumoured that lice spread the typhoid. We searched our hair and clothes thoroughly for lice, but the infestation got worse every day – this was one battle we could not win.

The atmosphere at that time was a strange mixture of fear and despair. We no longer saw any overseers or camp administrators. Just a short time before, Marta Baumöhl had been stopped by one of the overseers and offered the post of housekeeper, with her son. Marta was bowled over. Why her? But the overseer was never seen again, and Marta herself caught typhoid during the epidemic that was raging around. Marta fell asleep for ever in her bunk next to us just before we were liberated.

Ivan, Zsigi and I all caught typhoid, and Zsigi stayed with us while he was critically ill. While we were still in quarantine after being liberated, we lost each other. However, later I found to my joy that he had been sent to a Swedish hospital after treatment in

Bergen-Belsen, where they did all they could to restore him to health. More than a year passed before Zsigi returned home to Presov, and even then he had not recovered fully.

April 1945

The camp had run out of water completely, and many prisoners just vegetated in a weak and apathetic state. Those who were reasonably mobile dragged themselves about and looked for relatives and friends who had arrived before or since we had.

"Zsuzsa", said a particularly thin, but still youthful-looking, wraith from Bratislava, "I think I saw your sister, Ilka, somewhere." "Where? Where? Which block?" I urged her to remember, but she could do nothing more than insist that it really had been my sister.

I became very agitated, first with joy, then with worry about the state I might find her in. I gathered up all my strength and took my very weak little Ivan's hand. We walked from block to block looking for "Auntie Ilka". As we went up and down the gangways between the stacked bunks, I called out everywhere: "I'm looking for Ilka Diamant, my sister, from Bratislava!". But there was never any reply to my desperate enquiry. Exhausted, depressed and hopeless, I decided to go back to our hut.

At the very last minute I caught sight of a figure on a top bunk. She was almost completely bald and her face was etched by disease and suffering. She looked down and called out in tears: "Zsuzsa, are you here in this hell, too?" I hardly recognised my sister, just her voice. Was it really my sister? I couldn't reply, but we threw our arms round each other, sobbing and wordless.

I only learned about the details of my sister's deportation much later. She and her husband, Dr Nikolaus Diamant, had been transferred from the Bratislava ghetto to a collection camp in Sered. They lived there in terrible circumstances for a little while longer, together with other families they knew. They hoped to escape the 'Final Solution'. However, their stay there was short-lived; the Sered camp was to be closed. To avoid immediate deportation, their only choice was to seek refuge in the mountains or hide in the forests and villages with the other ex-camp inmates. But an irresistible fate awaited the Diamant family, just as it did most of the persecuted. They were arrested and deported. My sister was incarcerated in Grossrosen camp, and my brother-in-law in Oranienburg, from whence he did not return. The emptying of Grossrosen camp was achieved partly by train, partly by cattle truck, and finally on foot.

So we were reunited with Ilka and were able to move her to our block. Compared with the horrors we saw in her block, I must admit that conditions in the children's block, where we were, were a bit better. On the day that Ilka joined us, we did still each receive a bowl of soup, and we had no idea that it would be our last. From now onwards there would be nothing at all, not to eat nor to drink. No liquid, no calories. Ilka lay there in total apathy and we were dying of thirst. Our legs were swollen and we slept for most of the time.

We used the latrines less and less, since we had nothing to evacuate. It rained once or twice, and when it did we managed to collect a little water and to dampen our fevered faces and cool them down. The swelling of Ivan's stomach went down, we were dehydrated and had difficulty breathing. Ivan's pulse, when I felt it from time to time, was irregular – sometimes fast and sometimes hardly discernible.

New transports from liquidated camps arrived all the time, but the number of inhabitants grew smaller daily. The prayer, "give us this day our daily bread, forgive us our trespasses, as we forgive those who trespass against us. . ." was no help to us. There was nothing, absolutely nothing to eat. We received no more rations – none at all – and we were too weak to go looking for food. The only guards to be seen were in the watchtower, but one elderly soldier did come right inside our block, and emptied out his pockets.

He brought us beetroot and we ate them without peeling them. What a wonderful feeling it was to have something in our stomachs for once.

Our strength had ebbed away completely. We could hardly walk and Ivan was reduced to crawling on all fours. Since we were so weak, the latrines seemed miles away and we could no longer reach them. And now came the lowest point. We were in a state of complete breakdown. We no longer had the strength to remove the corpses and many of us just lay on our bunks surrounded by our dead friends.

I can't remember any more what was happening in the bunks above us, since climbing up and down to them was now impossible. Our hut turned into a hell of groaning, laboured breathing, coughing, blood being coughed up, and, for many, the very last breaths being drawn.

The white flag

We had lost count of the days, but on 15 April 1945 someone shouted into the hut: "We are free; there's a white flag". Many of them wouldn't believe it, but I did, and I stood up carefully. I moved to the door as if in a trance, and there really was a flag. "Ilka, Ivan, we are free", I screamed with infinite joy. "Get up. Come and see."

We positioned ourselves in front of the block and looked at the miracle. The entrance gate was closed, but the watchtower was empty. We were no longer accustomed to glaring light and the daylight really hurt our eyes, but we continued to stare at the entrance. Something had changed out here in the open – all over the place lay dead bodies, in the ditches, piled against the walls, on the steps, everywhere dead bodies.

Suddenly there was a movement at the gate and a car with two officers in an unfamiliar uniform and an SS man drove in. "Did you notice, the SS man had no insignia?" No, we hadn't noticed. After a short time, the car drove off again and the gate closed. Was it possible? Was that liberation? A few of the stronger prisoners tried to open the gate, but it wouldn't move. The Germans had gone but we were still locked in.

In desperation a prisoner who had gone mad with hunger threw himself on the wire. It turned out that the electricity had been cut off, but the would-be suicide still had enough strength to end his life by other means: he slashed his artery with a piece of glass. He was not the only one whom hunger had driven mad. Knut Hamsun describes the lengths to which people can be driven to by starvation in his novel, 'Hunger'. I have never been able to reach the end of this book, but I can bear witness that hunger can drive some people mad, others insane, others to fantasise and hallucinate about tables laden with wonderful things to eat, which they could but not touch. "Don't take it away, don't take it away, leave it here," they screamed furiously and insanely, with the last bursts of strength they could muster.

So the electric fence had been turned off and a few people managed to climb over the barbed wire. Prisoners returned with potatoes and other things to eat, but only the stronger ones managed to grab these 'treasures'. We others, the weakest of the weak, were satisfied with the leftovers.

Nothing happened on 16 April, but the 'real' liberation came about on 17 April.

Liberation

By the time liberation came, Ivan was neither able to stand nor to walk, he dragged himself about on all fours. His legs and tummy were swollen and bore all the signs of oedema caused by starvation. At eight years old he weighed nine kilograms .

The first thing that the Royal Army Medical Corps did when they arrived, was to provide huge cisterns of water. We were unendurably thirsty, and they gave us copious quantities of preserves. We were given sardines, peas, beans, ham and eggs, all sorts of canned fish, dried figs and lots of other goodies.

The starving people seized on all this food and couldn't stop eating. However, their shrunken stomachs could not cope with this unaccustomed nourishment and, having been reduced to skin and bone, they died by the hundreds in unbearable pain and cramps through perforated stomachs.

The liberators had meant so well in giving us these generous rations, but had no experience of dealing with such starvation. How could they guess that the excellent food and generous quantities might have such a disastrous effect on starving people.

The only reason we escaped this dreadful death was that we didn't eat all the provisions we were given. We just couldn't imagine that there might be more to come after this and so we hoarded some of it 'just in case' for the hard times ahead.

My exaggerated planning was unnecessary, but luckily protected us from the horrible consequences of over-eating.

We were actually not aware of the hand-over of the camp to the Number 10 Garrison Detachment and to 113 Light Anti-Aircraft Regiment. What we noticed was not the presence of the British, but of drinking water. It was the tankers of drinking water which embodied and symbolised liberation for us.

When we saw the water tanker, we could control ourselves no longer. After a two and a half week thirst, if you don't count the rainwater from puddles, we used our final strength to rush towards the water containers. The only thing that concerned me was to get a mug of water, so that I could give Ivan a swallow to drink. The distribution of the water had been going on for some time, and I was afraid there would be none left. There was no way I was going to wait for the next water tanker to arrive.

I was just taking a long step forward in the queue, when a self-appointed leader, who was now directing operations, screamed at me: "don't push in, you horrible creature." With her stick she hit me hard on the ear, knocking me away from the tanker, and I collapsed in pain. However, I forced myself back on to my feet and I did manage to obtain some of the wonderful, cool, thirst-quenching water for Ivan and for me.

Not only did the British army react very fast in providing us quickly and regularly with water, hut they also sent at once for specialists to deal with the catastrophic consequences of starvation. They immediately distributed the 'Bengal Famine Diet', which was a fluid containing molasses and including glucose and salt. This diet had been successful in Bengal, India, some years before, and here in the camp saved hundreds, maybe thousands, of people who were nearly on the brink of the hereafter.

We now had water to drink, liquid and solid nourishment to eat and could wash in warm water. I began to recover within hours and was able to concern myself with the welfare of Ivan, Ilka and Zsigi. However, in other respects, many things remained unaltered. People were still dying around us all the time.

Grief and anger

All the SS men and women, except for Josef Kramer and Irma Grese, were ordered to help with the disposal of the bodies by the British command. Huge lorries were driven up and the formerly powerful SS men and women were forced to load them up with corpses and unload them into communal graves.

One lorry after another. A hundred, or perhaps even two hundred skinny, emaciated, maltreated bodies on every load, from morning to night. The SS soldiers were now suffering the same conditions and the same number of calories that we prisoners had had to manage on. From time to time the SS soldiers were allowed to rest for a short while, and were allowed to lie down on the ground, at the bottom of the communal graves.

As we watched the loading of the bodies, our hearts were filled with grief and anger and it was some tiny recompense to see that our erstwhile tormentors were now suffering just as we had done such a short time ago.

Each time a grave filled up – with exactly 5,000 corpses – a service was held and the grave covered in. Then on to grave number two, then grave number three. The British concluded that everything was going well, but too slowly. The typhoid epidemic had to take precedence over piety, and the British command had to take a decision that seems almost incomprehensible nearly fifty years later. This was to use a bulldozer, not to dig the graves, but to push the bodies into them. With hindsight, the world may understand that the word 'about' gives the clue to why this amazing action was taken with regard to the graves. Time was pushing on, and it was no longer possible to count the bodies. 'About' 5,000, 'about' 3,000, 'about' 7,000 – so it went on and on. How could anyone come to an exact total? The English chaplain strode from grave to grave, from service to service.

Snatched from the inferno

The language barrier between the British army and the prisoners was almost complete. My knowledge of English enabled me to find out what was to happen to us now.

"We are just converting the SS Officer school into a hospital", explained one English officer. "We have requisitioned thousands of beds, and ordered lots of new ones, and we will transfer you to a clean environment."

20 April was the day we were to move into the hospital, but there was a delay because there had been an air-raid on the camp. The attack was particularly perverse, not only because they were shooting at a liberated camp, but more so because it completely held up the arrangements that the Red Cross were making.

Six days after the raising of the white flag, and four days after the first water tankers arrived, we were still in our block. Together with Ivan, who was very very weak, and Ilka, completely sunk in apathy, I waited for the transfer to hospital. Nothing else was important. We just wanted the ambulance to come as soon as possible. At last the stretchers arrived. There was room for four people in each ambulance, and the ambulances rolled up ceaselessly. Children had priority, and Ivan held my hand tightly when they came for him, so that we succeeded in getting away in the same ambulance. It was a slow, bumpy ride, so as to avoid disturbing the contaminated dust. We saw Belsen camp disappearing into the distance through the rear window of the ambulance. At last we were safe. We had been snatched from the inferno.

How we got clean

They laid us naked on the stretchers and wrapped us in clean blankets. Our pathetic clothing lay on a dump in front of the huts.

We drove for approximately twenty minutes and were then lifted on stretchers into a washroom and on to a table. Two strong German nurses soaped us, scrubbed, washed and rinsed us down, our hair was washed (though not cut off), and then they started the procedure all over again.

All clean and wrapped up, we were taken into the hospital wards and put to bed, where we fell asleep, totally exhausted, but blissfully happy. Meanwhile the cleaning procedure continued at a great pace without a break.

The nurses had been forced to do this duty by the British, but some others volunteered to do this heavy work. As it soon turned out, it was dangerous work – many of the nurses, working continuously, caught typhoid and died.

We awoke in soft, clean beds, in surroundings which looked human again. Outside, just a few kilometres away, the dying was continuing. Here in the hospital, every human life was worth something; we were looked after, cared for, human beings once again.

Hospital in Bergen

Ivan was still with me when I arrived at the hospital. However, when I was able to take stock of my surroundings from my lovely soft bed, I noticed that he was no longer there. When I asked the nurses where my son was, they looked at each other and whispered: "She's delirious". However, I insisted obstinately that I had had my child with me till we got to the entrance and urged them strongly to find out where he might have been taken by mistake in all the commotion, and please to bring him to me immediately.

Now we were only being given pure water or tea, or whatever we wanted, to drink, rather than coffee with bromide in it. We were once more members of the human race, with feelings, able to reflect, worry, and overcome by sad thoughts and deep unhappiness.

I worried day and night about whether my son, reduced to skin and bone as he was, might wake up in the strange environment of his hospital room, with nobody taking any notice of his complaints...would he even recover from his critical illness? Many people were dying in the hospital, unable to survive in their weakened condition.

I knew my sister was in the same hospital, but where? I didn't know which room she was in, and there was no way I could get out of bed to go and find out. An English Red Cross delegation came by to check on the organisation of the hospital. They stopped beside my bed to ask me how I was and whether I had any requests.

I replied to them in English, explaining my situation in tears, and begging them to find my child and bring him to me. Once again, with an evocative gesture, the nurses implied "She's delirious".

A few days passed, and my fever remained constant at over 40°, so it was hardly surprising that everyone thought I was imagining things.

By chance I realised that one of the orderlies was Hungarian. I promised him the world if he could find my little son somewhere in the hospital. There were only a few children among the survivors and I asked the orderly to talk to his child patients in Hungarian, and to ask them if their name was 'Ivanko'.

A few more days passed and I never stopped worrying. Suddenly my door opened, and what did I see? Wearing a sky-blue nightshirt, which I can still see in my mind's eye, there was my little, very pale Ivan in the arms of that wonderful Hungarian nurse. We both expressed our joy at being together again by non-stop quiet sobbing. He still had a temperature and was very weak, but I had him back!

I kept him with me in my bed and we remained like that until we were transferred to the convalescent home.

Mostly we were fed on tea, soup and biscuits. Our stomachs could not take more solid food. Our medical and clinical treatment were excellent, and, gradually, we began to get well.

May 1945

As soon as we were able to think straight, we were overcome by terrible worry about members of our family. We were desperate for news about what was going on in the world. Who was still alive? Who had survived unscathed? Who had been arrested and transported after us? How had Presov fared in further air-raids? We were very concerned about our home town of Presov, which had already suffered quite a lot of bomb-damage, including the orphanage where my children had found shelter, before our deportation.

The weeks passed in worry and hope. Those who were improving were re-housed in convalescent homes, which were converted from barracks into comfortable living quarters from one day to the next. These were maintained by German women who had volunteered. They wanted to help, but also to relieve their consciences, for they 'knew nothing about anything'. There we lived together, Ilka, Ivan and I.

A few people had reacted very oddly to convalescence, especially the younger prisoners who had lost any restraint during their long years of imprisonment. They became very vengeful and aggressive. Despairing over the endless suffering, degradation and loss of their families, they often took the law into their own hands and avenged themselves on the Germans. They formed gangs to go on raids all around, demolishing the private property of people whom they judged to be guilty of this tragedy. They destroyed everything that came into their hands.

Order was then restored by the British military authorities. No-one was punished, since it was understood that this was a psychological reaction to their suffering and that they were responding to insanity with insanity.

There were great celebrations on 8 May 1945, the end of the war. The anthem of each nationality was played. Each group listened to its own national anthem. I was moved as I heard the Hungarian, Czech and Jewish national anthems. Which one was my own? I didn't know, and I still don't know today.

I was able to make good use of my knowledge of languages. I translated from Hungarian, German, Slovakian and English. I understood Belgians, Dutch people, and even the Gypsies. My pharmaceutical training was of use in giving information to patients in the hospital, as I was able to translate the medical terms. In general, everyone used his or her professional skills. Dressmakers made sheets into wearable clothes, and cobblers and hairdressers were professionally active. We had no money, but textiles, cosmetics, preserves, and whatever we received from the British, formed the new currency, with much brisk bartering going on.

We had 'organised' a small milk-jug from somewhere, and Ivan, who was able to walk upright once again and wore comfortable, airy sandals instead of tight boots, fetched milk for us from the Officers' mess. They liked to spoil him, so they always gave him plenty. He could have anything he wanted – chocolate, raisins, chewing gum.

On one occasion a delegation from Sweden came to examine the living conditions of people liberated from Bergen-Belsen. Each of the few surviving children was asked if he or she had a wish. Most of them wanted a drawing-pad and crayons, as did Ivan. The drawing that he then completed was shown to a visiting commission. They thought my son was so talented that they suggested that I should take him to Sweden, where he would be taught drawing and painting. They thought it would be a pity not to encourage his talent.

However, I would not hear of it. We were waiting eagerly and impatiently for the time when we would be well enough to travel. Our only wish was to go home, go home, go home.

Actually many countries offered to take a few hundred liberated prisoners, but Sweden was the most generous – 6,000 people made their new home there.

At that time we were convinced that we would find at least some of the family at home. Gradually we began to gain strength and put on weight, thanks to the good and plentiful food. In our minds we were already at home. Shivering and often crying in anticipation and joy, we dreamt of the moment when we would be able embrace the loved ones we had cherished in our thoughts.

June 1945

Towards the end of June 1945 we informed the authorities that we felt fit to travel and wanted to go home. We left Bergen-Belsen with light hearts and travelled back through a bombed-out and destroyed Germany to Czechoslovakia. Our arrival in Presov was much more distressing than we had imagined. Seventeen of our closest relatives were missing, including my husband, my eldest son, Paul and my mother.

Nearly fifty years have passed since then, but the loss of my dearest ones is a wound that never heals. I shall remember those events till my dying day. I cannot – and do not want to – ever forget them.

Instead of an Epilogue

1945 *Homecoming*

Leave Belsen in July 1945.
Greeted with flowers in Pilsen, the first stop after the German/ Czech border.
Continue journey to Prague. Arrive in Prague on 14 July. Repatriation office. Given first money and ration books. Clothes from UNRRA.
Stayed in YWCA hostel in Prague.
Many notices on noticeboard:
I'M LOOKING FOR MY WIFE . . . , I'M LOOKING FOR MY HUSBAND . . . , I'M LOOKING FOR MY SISTER . . .
Nobody is looking for us.
Travel on to Bratislava.
Stay in Hotel Dachs.
Here we find out the hard facts – who is definitely dead, who may still return, and who is already at home.
My sister Magda and her daughter Susi have survived.
Ilka's husband is dead.
Trains are irregular.
Arrive in Presov on 27 July 1945 after many delays and changes.
Taken in by Magda.
The first person I saw in the street was the guard to whom I had given all my money in the Gestapo prison in November 1944. He stared at me as if turned to stone, stepped back and then disappeared from Presov.

For the first few weeks and months I am supported by the hope that my eldest son, Paul, might arrive back on one of the transports returning home. But he never did come back.

My main aim in life is to restore Ivan to health.
Ivan travels to the High Tatras several times for medical treatment.

72

1946 *Our own home*

Ivan started school in February 1946. He had missed the first and second years, but went straight into the third year because of his very good entrance exam results.

I go back to work at the Salvator Pharmacy, but I can't stay there. Bouts of crying and sleepless nights. If someone comes into the the pharmacy in uniform, I see the Gestapo in front of me.

I start a new career – private language teacher. The flexible hours allow me to give Ivan the attention he needs for the restoration of his health.

1947 *Ivan gets back to a normal childhood*
Joins the boy-scouts; new friends.

1948 *Karlsbad, Prague*
To my great surprise and joy, while on holiday in Karlsbad, by chance I meet Gabriel Sommer, an engineer from Bratislava, who is an old colleague from my student days. We had been close friends at Prague University, while students 20 years ago. He had wanted to marry me, but by the time he asked me, I was already engaged to Dr Lefkovits. Gabriel Sommer had remained single and the war had spared him and his family. One year after we met in Karlsbad we were married.

1956 *Ivan passes his school-leaving exams*
He registers at Prague University and studies chemistry.

1960 *Ilka emigrates to Australia with Arthur Silvan*
In 1961 Ivan graduates in chemistry and applies to the Czech Academy of Sciences in Prague.
In 1962 he marries his fellow student, Hana.
In 1963 my grandson, Michael, is born.

1963 *Ivan is awarded a UNESCO-Euratom fellowship and goes to Naples.*

In 1967 Ivan and his family leave Czechoslovakia for good. Ivan takes up a post at the Paul-Ehrlich Institute in Frankfurt am Main.

1968 *My husband and I emigrate.*
At the age of 65 my husband gets a good job as a patent lawyer at the German Metal Company in Frankfurt on Main.

1969 *Ivan and his family move to Basel*
He is a founding member of the Basel Institute for Immunology, founded for and directed by Professor Niels K. Jerne.
In 1974 we move to Freiburg im Breisgau when my husband retires at the age of 70.
In 1979 my husband dies of a heart attack while in the best of health. For thirty years of marriage he was a dear, good husband, and a loving, caring father for Ivan. He was always a positive influence on his development and whole way of life.

1984 *I move to Bettingen, where Ivan and his family live*
In 1986 I decide to write my 'memoirs' after a kidney operation. The first version is written in Hungarian, and I gradually translate the chapters into German.

1992 *I celebrate my 88th birthday in Prague with Ivan and his family*
It is a wonderfully stimulating and festive few days. A deeply moving farewell party to celebrate my Prague years, at which I mull over the first and second halves of my life, making me happy, sad and thankful – despite everything.

How accurate is this book?

My 'memoirs' have gone through several stages of development, and this one differs quite a lot from the original version.

Firstly, the original text was in Hungarian, which is the language in which I can express myself best. While I was writing the German text, I made a few alterations, and I actually like this version better than the original.

Secondly, I wanted to take account of the multitude of comments which I had received from friends, when they read the original text. I made various changes as a result of their suggestions and incorporated them into the German version. To give one example of this, I would like to refer to the chapter in which I describe the days I spent 'in bed' at the home of Katica Svaton. The description of events at that time is exact, but I made use of the opportunity to add a few words about my family, not only 'who is who', but also 'who is where', since they had all scattered in flight.

Thirdly, I was keen to avoid inaccuracies and obvious mistakes. My son, Ivan, was very helpful here, but also extremely strict. As far as was possible, he checked and researched all my statements, and if I had to admit that I was only relying on memory for something, he advised me to leave it out. Here is one example: I describe the death march from Ravensbrück to Bergen-Belsen exactly as it was. I remember walking the whole way, but Ivan got out the atlas and showed me that it could not have been possible. We must have travelled some of the way by train or lorry. So we asked Zsigi Baumöhl. He had been evacuated from Ravensbrück to Bergen-Belsen two days before we were and is convinced that they travelled by cattle-truck.

There are some other inaccuracies. These concern events where I was not present, such as the chapter in which I describe the death of my mother. And even Ivan, that guardian of accuracy, is unable to remember more about his stay in Budapest than what appears in the chapter 'a completely altruistic benefactress'.

It took much longer than I imagined it would to turn these 'memoirs' into the form of a little book that the reader could hold in his hands. But then I have stayed alive longer than I ever imagined too.

On my 85th birthday my son gave me a computer. I thought he was completely mad, since I imagined it would be impossible ever to master this machine. But the goal of finishing these 'memoirs' was such a strong motivating force, that I really did manage to learn how to use it.

We have reached 1994. Persecution began over half a century ago, so it is understandable if memories of a few events have become clouded. This is not an accurate historical document. I simply wrote my 'memoirs' as a final gesture in order to honour the memory of those members of my family who did not survive persecution.

A word of thanks

I should like to thank Dr Elisabeth Peterson, of Staufen, Germany. I owe her much gratitude for her great, and very useful, assistance with the translation of my 'memoirs' from Hungarian into German. I must thank all the friends who helped me get the book together, Mrs Magda Stitny, Mr André Wollner and all the others whose positive input into the then embryonic book, encouraged me to continue when I was hesitant. I must mention: Dr and Mrs Alexander Gordon (Basel), Professor and Mrs Desider Grünberger (New York), Mrs Anne Schlesinger (London), Mrs Klara Weisstaub (Haifa), Dr Agata Pilat (Prague), Professor Tibor Diamantstein (Berlin) and Dr Jehuda Lahav (Tel Aviv and Budapest).

Today the world asks us to 'forgive and forget'. I can only forgive on behalf of myself alone, not the millions who were done to death. Time is supposed to help with 'forgetting', but is not always successful.

But I will end my description of these terrible crimes with special thanks. There were countless ordinary people whom we did not know, who reinforced our belief that humanity and decency had not quite died out through their simple, but in those times, extremely dangerous good deeds.

And I should like to express my gratitude once more; I want to thank the unit of the British army that liberated us, just hours from death. I am aware that the army's heroics took place elsewhere, but that first water from the tanker, the move to hospital, the competence and compassion shown by one and all, taken together were balm to our maltreated souls.

I also wanted to thank my son Ivan, but he censored me here. Instead, I should just like to point out that it was Ivan who 'forced' me to write it down. I am sure his intention was to stimulate activity in my brain by means of psychological work therapy, so that I wouldn't succumb to old age. But I am placing on record at the end of this note of gratitude, that this book would not have come to fruition without Ivan.

Index of names mentioned in my 'memoirs'

Monsignor Mark Altmann, died in Ravensbrück. His wife and daughter survived.

Marta Baumöhl, née Sommer, died of typhoid in Bergen-Belsen.

Dr Zigmund Baumöhl, referred to as Zsigi in these 'memoirs', who was seven at the time, is now a practising doctor in Effretikon, Switzerland.

Dr Hugo Benedek, a Presov vet, survived with the rest of his family. Died after the war. *Mrs Benedek* lives in Presov with her son, *Juraj*.

Marta Blazek, a single woman in Presov.

Maria Boros and her husband, *Sandor*, attorney at the Tatra Bank in Presov, both died in Ravensbrück.

Sarlotte Brody and her daughter, from Presov. Both survived.

Dr Samuel Duschnitz and his wife committed suicide when they were arrested in Presov in November 1944.

Madame Elise, hairdresser, lived with her 94 year-old mother in the flat where we found refuge. Was deported at the same time as we were and died in Ravensbrück.

The *Engländer* sisters and their niece, *Agata Berner*. *Anna*, the eldest sister, died in Ravensbrück.

Lorant Fésüs, pharmacist, was shot by the Nazis in Kremnica (Slovakia), together with his wife and two children, *Paul* (14) and *Katica* (7).

Klara Fischer, niece of *Dr Friedmann-Mayer* and then a young girl, is now married to *Mr S. Weisstaub* and lives in Haifa.

Dr Ilonka Friedmann-Mayer, paediatrician, survived Auschwitz, emigrated to Israel after 1968, and died in 1992 aged 88.

Dr Elisabeth Grosswirth-Weiner and her two daughters.

Mr and Mrs György were the friends with whom my husband escaped to Budapest. They survived.

Mrs Kissoczy, nee *Csatary*, wife of the homeopathic doctor in Presov.

Dr Jehuda Lahav (Stephen Weiszlovits), journalist, lived for several decades in Israel, but now working in Budapest.

Vera Markus, then 14 years old. Survived. Teaches gymnastics and now lives in Budapest.

Mrs Mayer from Bratislava survived.

The doctor's wife, *Mrs B. Müller*, 'beauty queen', died of dysentry in Ravensbrück.

Dr Ludovit Pfeiler, owner of the Presov pharmacy when I last worked there, was a member of the German Party.

Dr Odon Propper, my mother's cousin, lives in Budapest with his family.

Mrs Olga R, an unmarried lady whose aim in life was to help refugees. She died of TB after the war.

Dr and Mrs Theophil Rosenberg, of Presov. Both died.

Manci Skalny helped many people, lived in Bratislava, and now in Cologne.

Serene Sommer, Marta Baumöhl's mother, died of dysentry in Ravensbrück.

Josef Stracensky, dental technician, to whom we owe a great deal, lives in Presov.

Katica Svaton, single and a dressmaker, lives in Presov.

Peter Titus, the priest who baptised us in Presov, is presumably dead.

'*Walter*', a young refugee from a Rumanian transport, hid in the same place as we did and presumably died.

Desider Weiszhaus, an engineer, and his wife, *Ilonka Grün* and son, *Jani* (15), died in Ravensbrück.

A note about the photographs

With some hesitation I have taken on the task of writing a few words to accompany the pictorial documentation. Up till now the reader has been used to 'little Ivan', and these lines from a grown-up Ivan might possibly spoil things. However, it is necessary to provide a short commentary on the background to my research on the photographs.

While my mother was choosing family photographs for the book, she bemoaned the fact that a happy world seemed to beam out of the pictures, which sat ill with the content of the book. I offered to do some research on photographic documentation of Bergen-Belsen, since I was sure that the pictures taken of us at the time of our liberation by the British army must be stored in an archive somewhere. My colleague, Peter Lachmann, Professor of Pathology in Cambridge, put me in touch with Mr Brad King, of the Imperial War Museum Film Department in London. I discovered from Mr King that there are seventeen reels depicting events in the first few hours of the liberation of the camp. Mr King reserved the film projection-room for me and I was able to watch the films in July 1992.

My wife came to London with me, as she wanted to be near me. She was not sure what effect reliving those events might have on me.

I watched all the films, often stopping them, noting positions on the picture sequences (for reproduction later), and I completed my overview of the whole horror within three days.

I recognised practically everything, and it was awful, indescribably awful – but I was still able to view all of it without being overcome. But that wasn't all. The more the film sequences progressed, the more impassioned I became. I couldn't stop until I had seen everything – some of the reels over and over again.

At the time we were too weak and apathetic to worry about anything other than our hunger and thirst. Now I had the opportunity to see everything. The camera swung from left to right and back again and it was as if I was there. When we were there we watched the SS loading up the lorries with corpses, under supervision of the British, but we never knew where they took them. Now I could see it.

In addition, we were too ill then to absorb the fact that the camp was burnt down. Now, with heart beating, I could witness this event and interpret it as the destruction of evil.

This documentation of the whole was not the only thing I saw. I also found something personal – a photograph of my mother and her sister, Ilka. Their faces are so disfigured, that it was more a case of presentiment, than actual recognition of their identity.

That is really all I want to say about the collection of this pictorial documentation. Perhaps just one more thing: the huge numbers of deaths did not stop with liberation; thousands died every day, then, later, hundreds, and at last the day came when no-one died. There was one sequence of pictures showing the hospital entrance. On the wall was a notice written in chalk: 'Today was the first day on which nobody died'. And they celebrated that event. Life and death had returned to their normal proportions.

Ivan Lefkovits

7. Bergen–Belsen Concentration Camp
    The board reads:
    THIS · IS · THE
    INFAMOUS BERGEN-BELSEN CONCENTRATION CAMP
    Liberated by the British Second Army on 15 April 1945
    10,000 UNBURIED CORPSES WERE FOUND HERE.
    13,000 MORE HAVE DIED SINCE THEN
    VICTIMS OF THE NEW GERMAN ORDER
    IN EUROPE AND ILLUSTRATION
    OF NAZI IDEOLOGY.

8.   Concentration Camp commandants
     Irma Grese and Josef Kramer after their arrest.

84

At the time we were liberated, dead bodies lay everywhere:

9.   on the paths . . .

10.   in piles . . .

11.   in the woods.

12. The most important symbol of freedom: water.

13. Potatoes being peeled.
     All still in the hopeless and contaminated camp.
     Still no division between the survivors and the dead.

14. The corpses were loaded onto lorries.

15.   SS men and women carried the corpses to the graves.

16.   The grave is full; exactly 5,000 bodies.

17.   They held a service and closed the grave.

18. From time to time the SS men were allowed to rest for a few minutes on the floor of the communal grave.

19. Piety had to give way. A typhoid epidemic is in full swing.
    The dead must be buried.
    They are pushed into the grave by a bulldozer.

20. The mayors of Celle and surrounding communities are ordered to come and look at the graves.

21.   Waiting to be transferred to hospital:
       my sister, Ilka (right) and me (middle).

22.   We are carried out of the huts on stretchers.

23.   The ambulance is waiting.
       On the right, the clothing which is left here in a heap and later burnt.

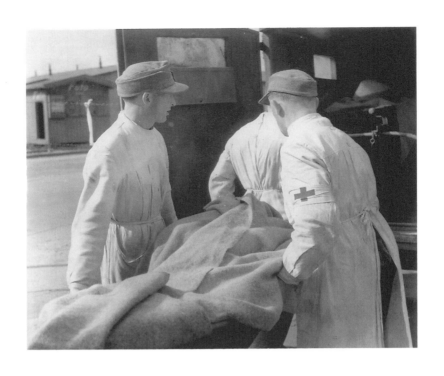

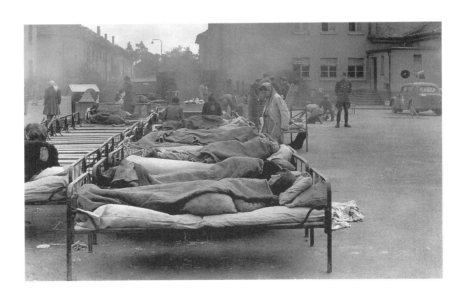

94

24.   We are carried into the ambulance.

25.   Waiting to be taken into hospital.

26.   We are deloused and disinfected.

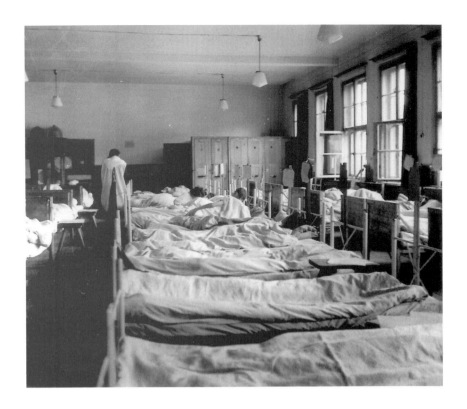

27. The washrooms – human laundry.

28. Whatever it is, special dietary food or calorie-rich soup, we get it very quickly and it is very good.

29. SS Officers' School, converted into a hospital.

30.   Wonderfully soft, clean beds.

31. Ninety-six medical students from England helped with the evacuation to hospital.

32.   Burning the contaminated Belsen camp.
      We did not see this with our own eyes. We were in hospital one
      kilometre away.

33.   They held celebration ceremonies, with many spectators:
      The British army, Red Cross and ex-prisoners who were strong
      enough.

34. The children recovered quickly.
    Drawing was not only a vital means of expression for the children, but
    also helped comprehension in this multi-lingual community.

35. These children had lost their parents.
    British soldiers made playgrounds for them.

36. Orphans two months after liberation.

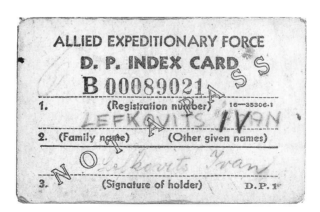

37. Our view of German towns through which we passed on our home-
     ward journey.

38. An important document: identity card provided by the garrison
     headquarters of the Allied Expeditionary Force.

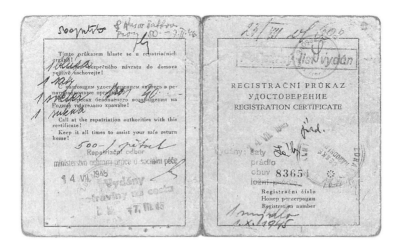

39. Ivan's and my repatriation papers. They are littered with many stamps
and include the statement that, among other things, we had received
one dress, one pullover, underwear, shoes and provisions for our
journey. They were probably issued on 7 July 1945 by the Czech
authorities.

COMITÉ INTERNATIONAL DE LA CROIX-ROUGE *Abgelegt*

SERVICE INTERNATIONAL DE RECHERCHES
3548 Arolsen · République fédérale d'Allemagne

INTERNATIONAL TRACING SERVICE   INTERNATIONALER SUCHDIENST
3548 Arolsen · Federal Republic of Germany   3548 Arolsen · Bundesrepublik Deutschland

HH   Téléphone: Arolsen (05691) 637 · Télégrammes: ITS Arolsen

Arolsen, den 2.September 1970

An den
Herrn Regierungspräsidenten
Darmstadt
Entschädigungsbehörde Wiesbaden

62 W I E S B A D E N
Postfach

Unser Zeichen   Ihr Zeichen
T/D - 962 793   D/ 52 368

Betrifft: LEFKOVITS, Ivan, geboren am 21.1.1931 oder 1937 in Presov

Sehr geehrte Herren!

Der nachstehende Bericht ist eine offizielle Ergänzung unserer Inhaf-
tierungs- und Aufenthaltsbescheinigung Nr. 481396 vom 4.Juli 1968:

LEFKOVITZ, Ivan, geboren am 21.1.1937, Staatsangehörigkeit: tschechoslowakisch,
wurde am 28.November 1944 von Preschau/Slowakei in
das KL-Ravensbrück eingeliefert, Häftlings-Nummer 88742
Kategorie oder Grund für die Inhaftierung: "polit." (politisch)
                                           "Jude".

Geprüfte Unterlagen: Zugangsliste des KL-Ravensbrück.

Hochachtungsvoll
Im Auftrage

A. Opitz

40. & 41.

The Red Cross International Missing Persons Bureau, based in
Arolsen, Germany, has jurisdiction over vital archive documents
pertaining to the Second World War. We wanted to make as complete
a list as possible of our relatives, friends and acquaintances. All we
were able to obtain was a few bare details about ourselves.

106

SERVICE INTERNATIONAL DE RECHERCHES
INTERNATIONAL TRACING SERVICE
INTERNATIONALER SUCHDIENST

D - 3548 AROLSEN

Tel. (05691) 6037 - Telegr.-Adr. ITS Arolsen

| Notre Ref
Our Ref T/D - 284 185
Unser Az | Votre Ref
Your Ref - - -
Ihr Az | Arolsen, den 8. Juli 1937 |

EXTRAIT DE DOCUMENTS	EXCERPT FROM DOCUMENTS	DOKUMENTEN-AUSZUG
Il est certifié par la présente que les indications suivantes sont conformes à celles des documents originaux en possession du Service International de Recherches et ne peuvent en aucun cas être modifiées par celui-ci.	It is hereby certified that the following indications are cited exactly as they are found in the documents in the possession of the International Tracing Service. It is not permitted for the International Tracing Service to change original entries.	Es wird hiermit bestätigt, daß die folgenden Angaben den Unterlagen des Internationalen Suchdienstes originalgetreu entnommen sind. Der Internationale Suchdienst ist nicht berechtigt Originaleintragungen zu ändern.

Nom / Name / Name **LEFKOWITSCH -/-**

Prenoms / First names / Vornamen **Paul -/-**

Nationalité / Nationality / Staatsangehörigkeit **tschechoslowakisch**

Date de naissance / Date of birth / Geburtsdatum **1.5.1930 -/-**

Lieu de naissance / Place of birth / Geburtsort **nicht angeführt -/-**

Religion / Religion / Religion **nicht angeführt -/-**

Noms des parents / Parents' names / Namen der Eltern **nicht angeführt -/-**

Profession / Profession / Beruf **nicht angeführt -/-**

Dernière adresse connue / Last known residence / Zuletzt bekannter Wohnsitz **nicht angeführt -/-**

Etat civil / Marital status / Familienstand **nicht angeführt -/**

Arrêté le / Arrested on / Verhaftet am **nicht angeführt -/-** in **nicht angeführt -/-** par / by / durch **nicht angeführt -/-**

Emprisonné / Confined / Eingeliefert **in Konzentrationslager Ravensbrück -/-**

No de détenu / Prisoner's No / Häftlingsnummer **12477 -/-**

Le / On / Am **siehe Bemerkungen -/-** venant de / coming from / von **nicht angeführt -/-** par / by / durch **nicht angeführt -/-**

Categorie / Category / Kategorie **"Jud." (* Jude) -/-**

Transféré / Transferred / Überstellt **am 4. April 1945 zum Konzentrationslager Ravensbrück/Schonungslager Mittwerda. -/-**

Indications complémentaires / Further indications / Weitere Angaben **keine -/-**

Remarques du SIR / Remarks of the ITS / Bemerkungen des ITS

Nach den Feststellungen, die wir treffen konnten, wurde die Häftlings-Nummer 12477 des Konzentrationslagers Ravensbrück zwischen dem 11. Novemb und 28. November 1944 ausgegeben. -/- "Mittwerda" (ein vermeintlicher Ort war ein Deckname, der seitens der SS verwendet wurde, um eine Vernichtung aktion in der Gaskammer zu tarnen. -/- Abweichungen der Anfrage siehe Rüc seite

C. Biedermann
Direktor

K. Greulich
für die Archive

A-143.1 * Explication du SIR, * Explanation of the ITS, * Erklärung des ITS

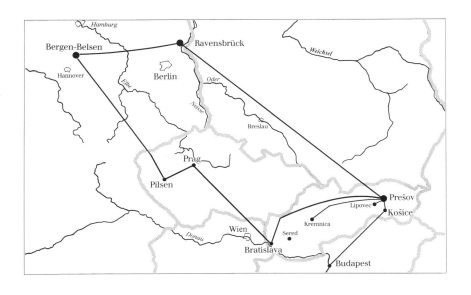

42. Route taken during our persecution. Starting with Presov, including
the two concentration camps, Ravensbrück and Bergen-Belsen.

Afterword: Countering the Fascination of Terror

Another holocaust story; we've seen them on TV, we've had eye-witness accounts, trials. Is there any more to be said on this subject? This was the question which raised itself when I began to deal with Elisabeth Sommer-Lefkovits' reminiscences. Any journalist has to ask that question quite coldly and cynically. Even more cynically - hasn't the fascination, the release, caused by the sheer unbearable depiction of the great horror, worn off long ago when it comes to the persecution of the Jews? And I remembered that, even when I was a child after the war, photographs of Jewish mass graves were the next favourite swap items to billion-Mark notes. While parents kept silent or spoke out, we children preserved the inconceivable like something forbidden.

At the same time as I was dealing with Mrs Sommer's reminis-cences, by pure chance the '*Basler Zeitung*' received a package from a Mr Jürgen Graf by the same post. Graf runs the Guideon Burg publishing house in Basel. This package contained the so-called Rudolph Judgement, the so-called Leuchter Judgement and an unpublished study on "the hypothesis that Treblinka was a techni-cal necessity", by an engineer called Arnulf Neumaier, from Riederau in Germany. Enclosed with this package was a letter from Jürgen Graf, with the undisguised exhortation finally to put right the history of the holocaust in the press – for the sake of scientifically proven truth. The 'truth' about the holocaust is that no such 'truth' ever existed.

The purpose is clear and it makes one more than angry. That is how revisionist legal intellectual property is disseminated to people under the guise of scientific neutrality. The goal is publicity at all costs – even if it is critical. And because the newspaper understood his motivation, nothing at all was published. I have no wish to dwell on it further; just to say this: to read between the lines of these 'judgements' is just as fascinating as to read about the horror. Scientific jargon is used for purposes of concealment just like dreadful bureaucratic language of the Nazis.

Was it just chance that the package arrived at that very moment? No. The resurgence of Nazism on the the streets is accompanied on an intellectual level by a dangerous shifting of history. The flood of facts we have today can be manipulated very easily, and a receptive mind will always retain something; a pin will always stick. To counter this it is necessary to have the witness of personal memories; the more dreadful the experiences, the greater effect they will have. The more unbiased they are, the less they seem like a blanket indictment. Elisabeth Sommer's story convinces because she has managed to distance herself from her tragic history, but has retained an inner nearness to the people of those times. That is how to counter the fascination of horror – and hence the reason for this book.

Ewald Billerbeck